COMPUTERS
ON THE JOB

COMPUTERS ON THE JOB

Surviving Canada's Microcomputer Revolution

HEATHER MENZIES

James Lorimer & Company, Publishers
Toronto 1982

ISBN 0-88862-553-7 paper
     0-88862-554-5 cloth

Design: Don Fernley

Author Photo: Fred Chartrand

Canadian Cataloguing in Publication Data

Menzies, Heather, 1949–
   Computers on the job

1. Computers — Social aspects. 2. Computers — Economic aspects. 3. Automation — Canada. 4. Electronic data processing and industrial relations. 5. Job security — Canada. I. Title.

HD6331.2.C3M46   331.25'9   C82-094493-9

60, 642

James Lorimer & Company, Publishers
Egerton Ryerson Memorial Building
35 Britain Street
Toronto, Ontario M5A 1R7

Printed and bound in Canada

6 5 4 3 2   83 84 85 86 87

Contents

v

Acknowledgements

To the extent that this book proves useful to workers, managers, educators and policymakers, it will be due to the assistance and support I received from the following people: Carol Collier, Arthur Cordell, Linda Fischer, Gerald and Pat Haslam, Eric Manning, Katherine McGuire, Diane McKay, Jan Mears, Janet Menzies, Angus Ricker, George Sekely, Peter Warrian, Pat Webb, Russel Wilkins, Anthony Wilkinson and my good friend and husband, Miles Burton.

Preface

We are living through a second industrial revolution, propelled and shaped by the computer. This powerful new technology — particularly in the tiny, cheap form of the microchip — is transporting us from the mechanical age into the computer age. Just as the machines of the industrial revolution replaced manual labour and extended the power of muscles, so the computer is replacing — through automation — mechanical routine labour and extending the power of the brain.

In other words, while computers can lead to massive job losses through automation, they also herald a world of possibility literally made bigger by computer technology. For instance, none of the space program would have been possible without computers, which calculated the rockets' trajectory and thrust with an accuracy impossible with previous technology. In medicine, the CAT (computerized transverse axial tomography) scanner, which provides doctors with a three-dimensional "picture" of the brain, has greatly expanded the horizons of research into mental disorders and diseases of the brain.

When computers are combined with the equally powerful technology of communications — television, telex, telephones, cable, microwaves and satellites — they create an exciting new basis for work and activity in what is being called the information society. The problem is how to release the computer's potential for this new activity so that people being relieved of often boring jobs by automation can move ahead to new and more rewarding work creating the information society of the computer age.

The question is central to this book and to the history of technology in society. In ancient Greece, the philosopher Aristotle declared, "When the looms weave on their own, man will be free." However, the history of technology has been one of control more than one of liberation. For most people, being freed from the machines they work at can mean the misery of unemployment.

Technology has always been a powerful enabling factor, from the time people first made tools. It reached a zenith of influence with the invention of mass production machinery and the factories of the industrial revolution. When the skilled worker such as the weaver entered those factories, he lost not only control over the weaving process but even his status as a craftsman. The weaving craft was absorbed into the mechanical operations of the factory loom, which the factory owner, rather than the craftsman, now controlled. As a result, the job of weaver could be performed as easily by an unskilled child as by a skilled adult, and wages for weavers dropped accordingly — from thirty shillings a week to roughly five shillings. The weaver was reduced to competing with his own children for employment, and their employment was necessary to supplement the father's reduced income. Child labour became widespread because it was made possible and necessary by mass production technology.

It was a monstrous age, one of the maddest triumphs of technology over humanity. And, just to ensure that it worked effectively, fear of the poorhouse reconciled people to their virtual enslavement in factories, where they often had to stand from 5 in the morning to 9 at night.

But technology didn't create the industrial revolution; it merely provided the means for casting the values of the times into a set of social and economic relations. These values were themselves forged some time earlier, in the scientific and religious revolutions of the sixteenth and seventeenth centuries.

The Protestant Reformation enshrined both individualism as a virtue and personal gain or profit as its expression. The scientific revolution not only produced new technology, it also legitimized technique — the notion of applying science to a specific purpose. Mass production became the vehicle for expressing these new values and ideas, offering profit as the purpose to which technique could be harnessed. It also helped mould the market economy, which is simply a method for reducing all three factors in production — land, labour and resources — to a single common value expression, supply and demand. Once people were reduced to marketable units of labour, and land and resources were similarly given fixed value terms, these factors could then be bought and sold, and thereby controlled.

It's no coincidence that the spinning mule, invented in 1830, became the prototype machine for the industrial factory rather than the earlier spinning jenny. The spinning jenny enhanced the skill and work of the craftsperson, allowing the individual the freedom to do more, and to do better. The spinning mule, however, froze the craft of spinning into a series of mechanical parts that the factory owner controlled and turned to his own purposes. (It also enabled factory owners to substitute an unskilled, and therefore highly replaceable, labourer for the formerly indispensable craftsperson.)

It's worth reviewing the lessons of history as technology, in another peak of influence, introduces what is being variously labelled the computer revolution, the microelectronic revolution or the information revolution. It is also being called a second industrial revolution because, like mass production machinery before them, computers are transforming society, not just adding something to its traditional constitution.

Futurists, thinkers who try to interpret emerging trends, argue that the service sector, which emerged after the Second World War, is now being supplanted by what they call an information sector and an information society. People freed from dull jobs as "information workers," merely recording, reporting, filing and transmitting information, will become "knowledge workers" in this new society. They will *apply* information and automated information handling systems to create new wealth in wisdom. According to the descriptions of Alvin Toffler and other futurists, this information society will be a phantasmagorical fulfillment of Marshall McLuhan's richest expectations in the global village concept: a worldwide communications grid where electronic highways in the sky beam information via satellite and across cable, optical fibre and telephone lines. Everyone will be plugged into this dynamic, interactive intelligence universe through two-way television sets located at home or in the automated office.

In such a society, everyone would be a participating member, not just a consumer, in the computer communications system. "Work" (if the term were still necessary) would consist of creating knowledge of all kinds (hobby information on stamps, coins and so on, specialized research material, advice, counselling, philosophical discussion material, poetry) and selling or exchanging it through the open-ended marketplace of the electronic information system. In this scenario, librarians might create information materials for special-interest groups — on everything from ecology to archeology, medieval music to existentialism. Bank employees might tailor long-term investment plans to an individual's particular life plans and circumstances, where previously such customized work could only be cost-justified for large corporate customers. (What makes this all possible is the automation of the routine clerical and administrative support work of gathering, sorting, processing and orchestrating the relevant paper-based information.)

Factory employees might design customized products (cars, furniture, clothing), which automated manufacturing processes are making as economically feasible as mass production. Individual designers would advertise prototype designs and receive orders via the computer communications system.

This kind of future is possible. It requires concerted action, beginning with investment in innovative new opportunities for people to apply computer communications systems. As well, job-creating, job-enhancing support measures such as training and mobility assistance are needed.

Unfortunately, futurists seldom go beyond what computers *can* do, to explore what they *are* being employed to do. So far, the literature promoting automated systems for the office and factory stresses their "labour savings" potential and their utility for improving "productivity" and "fighting inflation." The message is to replace people with automated equipment to survive in today's society, not to build a new one.

And, as some companies are influenced by this bias, others are almost forced to copy them. One social forecaster in the United Kingdom predicted that 5 million Britons risk unemployment because of automation, but that 5.5 million could lose their jobs if British industries fail to automate and, as a consequence, go bankrupt.

Gordon Thompson of Toronto is one of the few futurists who question whether computer technology is being applied in a way that will stimulate new and enriched employment opportunities, and his conclusions aren't encouraging. He is convinced that the full flowering of the information society will require a shift in values and priorities. The current values behind information computer applications, he feels, are an extension of those that characterized the mechanical or industrial age. Expressed as such operating priorities as cost cutting and "concentrated benefit," these values are not only inappropriate to an information-based economy, Thompson argues, but they could actually suppress its development.

Consider the following, based on a forward projection of a few negative aspects of existing applications of computer technology. A travesty of the rich, open knowledge society, this future would feature only a few mass-produced information products, which would be consumed by the majority. This majority might be unemployed, or underemployed, with talent and skills left idle. At its bleakest, this scenario might rely on surveillance as a mainstay of employment in the information society. With everyone plugged in, everyone can be monitored easily.

The portends of such a scenario, however sensational, are already present. In addition to putting people out of work, computer technology is absorbing skills and control over the work process into machines and leaving many people with much simpler, even trivial, jobs to do. Computer monitoring is on the increase; examples include cashiers in supermarkets, whose performance is measured by the number of keystrokes per hour as they use their electronic cash registers. It's also happening to telephone operators and to machine operators in an Alberta mine, where computers control and monitor the use of machine instruments.

But the computer technology is still new. The challenge is to manage its application — through implementation guidelines, job creation, training, occupational bridging and other measures — to enable the promise of the computer age, the positive scenario, to be fulfilled, and in time.

Well, good luck, Benson. Do keep in touch and remember this little sacrifice is your contribution to the age of the chip.

Introduction

When forty-one telephone oper-
ators in the picturesque rural community of Ste. Agathe, Quebec,
lost their jobs through automation in 1981, they didn't know what
computers could do, nor that the automation process that would
take over their work had been going on for at least ten years; it
had merely taken that long to touch these women's lives. Similarly,
when General Motors installed its first robots on an Oshawa,
Ontario, auto assembly line, company management didn't anticipate that the fierce competitiveness introduced to the world auto
trade by Japan's use of robots would almost compel GM to un-
dertake a massive automation program. The company now plans
to have 14,000 robots throughout its North American factories by
1990.

These developments signal the enormous effect that computers
are having on our society. Their impact is being likened to a second
industrial revolution, not only because the technology is affecting

almost every industry and area of life but also because it is a transformative technology. While computers are automating countless activities — activities that currently provide employment for millions of Canadians — they also make possible countless new activities that could provide new sources of employment, if and when they are developed.

This book examines these two dynamics, from the points of view of individuals trying to adapt to the radically changing job market, of employers trying to improve productivity through automation and explore new computer-aided innovations, and of educators, union officials, policymakers and women's organizations trying to address the larger issues involved.

Chapter 1 looks at how computers have come to be such a powerful force in our society. It traces the history of the technology, with the aim of demystifying it, and examines the kind of work that computers can automate.

Chapters 2, 3 and 4 explore how computers are automating traditional work in offices, factories, banks, supermarkets and even sawmills. They examine the process of computerization from the automation stage through the integration stage and finally to the innovation stage, where new employment could emerge. Chapter 5 is devoted to the promising new information industries associated with the innovation phase. It looks at the technology as well as the corporate configurations involved. It also raises questions: about corporate concentration, freedom of information and privacy, and the limitations of the technology in a society that values human freedom and diversity.

The second half of the book is intended as a guide to the future. Chapter 6 describes the employment opportunities associated with the new information industries, in the traditional industries being transformed by computer technology and, as a third area, in developing and installing the technology itself. The chapter also includes job mobility scenarios both for employers trying to relocate redundant support staff and for individuals who have to make those moves on their own. Chapter 7 looks at the education and training required to survive the transition into the computerized work world and to develop careers within it. It also describes

2

the basics of computer literacy, which all Canadians will require in the years ahead.

The final chapter examines what needs to be done within the workplace, through collective agreements, labour legislation, job sharing and apprenticeships. It also explores VDT radiation and other issues that must be dealt with.

I'd love to be around when they get this thing perfected.

1
Computers, Chips and Automation

About half the work done in North America can be labelled "information work." However it's pigeonholed, as financial analysis, management, secretarial, sales and other services or even manufacturing, the work involves handling information — information that computers can handle for you, and possibly instead of you. But the use of machines to manipulate information isn't a product of the contemporary business world. Throughout history, people who needed to make tabulations, keep records or run manufacturing processes dealt with information, too — and looked for tools to make the work easier.

The humble abacus, pioneered by the Chinese six centuries before Christ, is the first well-known example of a tool that can store information as the altered state of a physical thing, which in turn can be manipulated. In this case, the altered state is achieved by moving the beads along the rods of the abacus. Today the same principle is applied in the computer, through electronic switches.

While this early calculator seems crude today, the abacus never-theless gave considerable power to its early users: the power of information.

Information at its simplest is difference. Black exists, for in-stance, because it is different from white. Similarly, a percentage communicates information because it expresses a difference be-tween the part and the whole. Numbers and letters are the building blocks of information. They are coded concepts for representing the reality we have observed. The code can be processed according to commonly accepted logical routines to yield insight, the power of being informed. Sometimes reducing our world to these codes is frustrating, like completing a multiple-choice questionnaire when the answer you want lies somewhere between boxes 1 and 2, or between 3 and 4. Information that won't fit into these boxes, such as nuances and subjective or qualitative information, is lost. Still, once information has been codified or, in computer jargon, dig-itized, it can then be processed automatically by the computer. This is what makes computers so important to jobs today: they can take over handling any information once it has been coded into digital symbols and entered into the computer as input data. Essentially the computer manipulates the data by following a fixed pattern of instructions (akin to a recipe or knitting pattern) spelled out in computer programs. This manipulation is called data pro-cessing, and a data bank is an electronic file where data is stored.

Between the heyday of the abacus and the advent of the modern computer came many innovators who sought to increase their information power. In 1642, the philosopher and mathematician Blaise Pascal, the son of a French tax collector, substituted toothed wheels for abacus beads in the world's first known mechanical adding machine. He also incorporated some of the manipulation routine, or program, into the machine itself. As numbers were dialled in on one of the interlocking wheels of the machine, the levers inside were set to trip a movement in the wheel representing the next order of magnitude (the hundreds were next after the tens, for instance). A speedometer runs on the same principle.

Charles Babbage, a British mathematician, made two significant additions to the computer's development. In 1822 he invented the difference machine, a calculator that set Pascal's principles to work on a scale never before dreamed of, by solving equations. It was really a special-purpose computer, limited to that one function. But Babbage still wanted a general-purpose machine. Instead of building a series of pattern-of-action choices into one machine, he went for the truly inventive. He designed a set of identical moving parts that could be manipulated to perform innumerable functions according to different patterns of action, equivalent to modern programs. Although it was never completely built, the analytical engine achieved the theoretical leap from calculating machine to programmable computer.

The analytical engine incorporated the five component parts, or functions, that are found in all modern computer systems. There were the input and output functions, which fed numbers and instructions into the mechanism and yielded the results as printed numbers. Inside, the arithmetic or processing function, which Babbage called the "mill," actually did the calculations. The store or memory function held numbers waiting to be processed. Finally, the control function or unit ensured that the machine completed all the calculations in the right sequence before going on to another task.

In planning the analytical engine, Babbage recycled from his difference machine the cogs and wheels to handle the calculation fucntions, the mechanical rods and levers to perform the memory functions and the numbered wheels for recording the information output. For the all-important input and control functions, he borrowed from the French weaver Joseph Jacquard, who in 1804 had automated the control function of a weaving loom.

Jacquard had designed a series of stiff cards with holes punched in them that corresponded to the intricate floral patterns being woven. At each throw of the shuttle, one of these cards was placed in the path of the rods, which were pulled forward to complete the weave. Where there were holes in the card, the rods slipped through; where there were none, the rods were held back. Card by card, each with its program of punched holes, the weaving pattern was created. In Babbage's analytical engine the punched cards replaced the hand-controlled levers for setting the calculation function in motion and controlled the sequence of calculations that the mill performed.

One contemporary observer — Lord Byron's daughter, Ada, the Countess of Lovelace, who was an intimate friend of Babbage's (his mistress, some say) — made some prophetic observations about the computer's role as an intellectual tool: "The Analytical Engine has no pretensions whatever to originate anything. It can do [only] whatever we know how to order it to perform. It can follow analysis; but it has no power of anticipating . . . any truths. Its province is to assist us in making available what we are already acquainted with."

The invention of electricity moved computers from the realm of the possible into that of the practical. In 1890, the American Herman Hollerith employed electricity in his tabulating machine, which was used for calculating the American census of that year. He used the punched cards Jacquard had pioneered and the idea of rods going through the holes. But instead of moving wool and silk threads into position to complete a weaving pattern, Hollerith's rods dipped into a bowl of mercury to complete an electric current that, in turn, caused a clock dial to advance by one turn. The success of this machine, able to "read" punched cards from the census returns, led to the formation of the Computing Tabulating and Recording Company, later renamed International Business Machines, or IBM.

The next developments were technical improvements, such as the use of vacuum tubes or electronic valves instead of electromagnetic relays for processing data. Electronic valves can perform hundreds or even thousands of data processing steps, called cycles, per second, while electromagnetic relays could only handle five or ten cycles per second. The first tube computer was the Colossus, developed by the British under a blanket of secrecy during the Second World War. By helping to crack the German intelligence codes, it is credited with helping to win the war for the Allies. This was but a preview of the vital importance information technology would assume in modern society.

Ironically, the Germans believed that their codes were impregnable because they were generated by an information-scrambling computer of their own invention, called the Enigma machine; but it had electromagnetic components. The British, with their faster vacuum tubes, devised a series of the codes and processed the

German information signals against them until, finally, intelligible data sequences appeared on the printout. The information was fed in on punched paper tape and "read" by a photoelectric reader that could absorb 5,000 characters per second, an impressive rate at that time. Then it was processed through 2,000 vacuum tubes.

An American computer, the ENIAC, boasted 19,000 vacuum tubes. Although it could only be reprogrammed by extensive re-wiring, it nonetheless was a stored-program computer, which was a significant development. Still, both machines were restricted to the role of glorified adding machines.

Another turning point was the development of the transistor, in 1947. The new invention replaced the vacuum tubes as the switching mechanism (logic gates) in the computer that actually processes data into information. It represented a dramatic new application of electricity: instead of moving an electric current, transistors registered difference by displacing a few electrons in a tiny globule of semiconductor material, which normally doesn't conduct electricity. The transistor consisted of layers of silicon, a semiconductor, that had been treated with impurities to make it conduct electricity across the areas that had been treated. This breakthrough greatly increased the reliability of computers and overcame the physical encumbrances of the vacuum tube computers. The process of getting computer equipment into progressively smaller spaces had begun.

Years later, when the planar oxidization process was developed for etching on these impurities to create the logic gates, which correspond to the possible choices in processing, the microelectronic revolution was launched. It became possible to etch several logic gates (or transistors) onto the surface of one piece, or chip, of silicon no bigger than a baby's fingernail.

The planar etching process started a war of miniaturization and economies of scale that popularized computer technology and left the ad writers scrambling for new and better descriptive labels. At first it seemed a miracle that one logic gate was etched on a chip. By the mid-1960s, though, these were replaced with small-scale integrated circuits, chips with ten or more logic gates. Then came medium-scale integrated circuits with hundreds of components. The early 1970s would see the manufacture of large-scale integrated circuits with thousands of components or logic gates per chip. The greater the miniaturization, the lower the price. The lower the price, the more information work computers could take on, and the more work functions could be automated.

Despite miniaturization, the computer in the 1950s and 1960s was still rather like the steam engine of the industrial revolution. It was big, clumsy and expensive. Just as the steam engine made it impractical to mechanize anything but large mass-production activities, so computers made it uneconomical to automate anything but large-scale production processes. The majority of installations in industry were in continuous-flow production processes, consisting of a series of interlocking standard steps or procedures, with the product literally flowing automatically from one place to another. Applications included smelting, oil refining, pulpwood processing, grain cleaning and brewing. Product handling, which included assembly work and inventory, could not be automated. Nor could most information handling.

What information-related work could be automated was originally confined to major statistical projects with massive data processing requirements, mainly in the tertiary or service sector of the economy. Governments installed computers for processing income tax returns and, later, payroll deductions and other data on their own employees. Airlines used them for tabulating airline reservations and cargo statistics. Banks installed them for processing cheques and calculating interest. Insurance companies used them to calculate and process insurance premiums. Companies in retail trade bought them to process sales-return data. Companies in the rail, truck and shipping business used them to process ticket sales and waybill data.

The first wave of computer automation slowly but surely had some major effects on both organizational hierarchies and the larger employment scene. When computers were first installed in the service-sector businesses, they were seen as something alien, and their operators were regarded with awe, if not suspicion. Initially, the work was distinctly alien as well; data processing was called "number crunching" and left at that. A sideline of the primary tasks in the office, it didn't really affect the regular office staff, who carried on their paper-based information work with only a touch of paranoia showing in the general disdain with which they regarded the "computer types."

The computer types, meanwhile, were steadily enlarging the scope of their information work. In manufacturing, they expanded from simple financial recordkeeping to inventory management and production scheduling. In service industries, they automated marketing functions such as sales and advertising feedback analysis. And in corporate head offices everywhere, they expanded into costing, cash-flow analysis and long-range forecasting and planning.

In their expansion, the computer types also created a whole hierarchy of new information occupations. The new positions ranged from systems analysts and designers, who drew up the general requirements of a data processing job or automation project, to computer programmers who translated these into orders the computer could follow, computer operators who ran the computer and data-entry clerks (originally keypunch operators) who fed the data into the computer.

Later, tape librarians and data network personnel were added to the hierarchy. Their jobs were to maintain and store the magnetic tapes full of data and to begin creating data banks, the electronic files of the office of the future.

Few people noticed the similarities between these occupations and those associated with a traditional office hierarchy of information workers. Yet the systems analysts and designers were obviously the equivalent of corporate planners, the computer programmers were akin to office managers and administrators, and computer operators, data clerks and tape librarians resembled secretaries, administrative assistants and other office support staff. One group worked with computerized or automated information systems; the other worked with print-based information systems. Neither group realized it was in competition with the other, and for the time being this redundancy was allowed.

The organizational shakeup that computers were to cause was not yet evident in the first wave era of the 1950s and 1960s, but there were predictions that computer automation would lead to mass unemployment. The catastrophe never materialized, because of the state of the technology, the state of the workplace organization and the state of the economy.

The first computers were just too big and, more to the point, too expensive, to push into all the nooks and crannies where people worked. This was particularly true of the emerging service industries — banks, insurance companies, telephones and other utilities. Although head-office statistical functions could be automated, a lot of the work, particularly in the branches, was widely distributed and rather unsystematic, not like work in processing industries, which was tightly organized, standardized and centralized. Also, since much of the work in service industries involved creating and handling information, which defied available productivity measures except when reduced to data for processing, it escaped productivity pressures. There was little pressure for productivity, in any case. The world economy was booming, and there was an abundance of people willing to work for relatively low wages.

Some of these were people being displaced by automation in the processing industries. But mostly they were women entering the paid labour force. The increasing participation of women in the paid labour force has been one of the most dramatic developments in the postwar era. Women doubled their participation rate between 1950 and 1980.

While the state of the economy kept predictions of widespread unemployment from coming true, the accompanying bullish state of mind also made people pay little attention to doomsayers. The 1960s were a time of confidence in technology and in society's ability not only to shape its collective destiny but also to generate more health and wealth for all. Meanwhile in scholarly circles there was a successful battle to redefine the industrial revolution as an unblemished triumph of technology, and an American presidential commission on automation concluded that technological change shouldn't lead to unemployment in any self-respecting economy. Quite the reverse was true: increased productivity produced by technological change will lead to increased economic activity, which will lead, in turn, to increased employment, it said.

The formula did not deal with the question of skill loss, which

12

has accompanied technological change since Joseph Jacquard invented his punch-card-controlled loom. Yet when automation was introduced to the pulp and paper, grain-cleaning and other processing plants in the 1950s and 1960s, the skill, knowledge and personal discretion associated with turning wood pulp into paper, cleaning grain and operating the other processing plants were absorbed into the computer-controlled machines. Employees who previously had been required to know the production process enough to fine-tune it, run chemical tests and adjust equipment were now reduced to bored machine operators watching dials and meters all day. The higher rates of alcoholism, drug abuse and absenteeism reflected the lowered job satisfaction of workers in these plants.

The formula also ignored possible jobless economic growth, and the problems associated with occupational mobility — the difference in skills and other qualifications between jobs being automated and new jobs created. The estimated 1.5 million people displaced when the processing industries were automated did not find new work in these same industries. Their unemployment just happened to coincide with the emergence of the new service industries, which could absorb them not because they had the right qualifications, but because few skills were required in most of the new jobs: driving trucks, buses and taxis, filling out forms, waiting on customers and the like.

How will this formula hold up in the second wave of automation, which arrived with the microprocessor in 1971? The first wave did not yield the terrible disruption predicted, because the economy was booming, because the technology had tight perimeters of application and because many large enterprises just weren't ready to automate. But now the economy is sluggish, more companies have standardized their operations and are looking for ways to cut costs, and the technology has few limits.

The microprocessor, a "computer on a chip," has allowed computers to go anywhere and automate almost any mechanical process. Packaged as tiny microprocessors, computers have become flexible, accessible and cheap. The microprocessor could be installed in this small corner to automate a minor control function or in that small corner to automate a recording function. It could also be incorporated into a hierarchy of computer control for maximum value per computer-power dollar. In terms of the hierarchies in any organization, the microprocessor and microcomputer are ideal for automating small local tasks such as filing, typing or parts assembly; at the equivalent of department management level, a medium-sized computer (a minicomputer, perhaps) can coordinate supplies, scheduling and other administrative functions automatically. Finally, at a senior management level, the traditional large computer (called a mainframe) can maintain overall control and supervision while monitoring and coordinating the entire operation.

In applicability, the difference between the original large computer and the versatile, cheap little chip is as profound as the difference between the steam engine and electricity. It is also as important to the spread of automation as electricity was to the spread of mechanization. When machines required an external power source such as the steam engine, it was feasible to mechanize only large mass-production activities — such as in manufacturing and processing plants. With electricity, however, mechanical power was incorporated into every conceivable mechanical process, not only in large factories but in small shops, farms and homes as well. Today all that a microprocessor needs is electricity, and it can be incorporated into almost anything that's already been mechanized. The cost of its power, roughly five dollars per chip in 1980, is declining at some 35 percent a year.

On farms, microprocessors incorporated into mechanical feeding systems can monitor and control the amount of chop being channelled from the silo into the feedlot. In homes, they can monitor the furnace, the humidifier and even the stove, and guard against break-ins. In office copiers, they can react to commands encoded in the information beamed to them from a word processor down the hall. In factories, they can monitor temperatures, test chemical solutions and control the arms of assembly-line robots. All told, it has been estimated (in *Business Week*) that nearly half of all jobs could be eliminated, deskilled or otherwise changed by the current second wave of automation.

Never before has one invention had such a widespread application. Nor has history recorded such a short time lag — less than ten years — between invention and adoption, or such a blinding rate of implementation. But microprocessor technology is called revolutionary for another, still more important reason: because of the transformation it triggers. It transforms by adding the dimension of "intelligence" — the capacity to inform and be informed. Equally important, and arising from its distributed-power characteristics, the technology of computers can be integrated with compatible technologies — such as telephones, cables and other communications systems. One of the most potent examples of this integration is called computer communications, or informatics. A combination of computer and communications technologies, informatics is creating a revolution in its own right.

Just what sort of future this new technology will create is being determined now in the way it's being applied. In the next three chapters we'll look at applications in offices, in service-sector business such as banks, insurance companies and stores, and in industry.

I do enjoy our Monday morning teleconferences. No matter how automated we get, the sycophants will always be with us.

2

The Automated Office

 he microprocessor is the long-awaited device being used to haul the office out of the nineteenth century, where it has languished in a disorganized flurry of meetings and paperwork, defying both measurement of productivity and means of improving it.

In a productivity drive that's affecting offices across the country, typewriters, dictating equipment, adding machines and filing cabinets — all introduced to the office a hundred years ago — are being tossed out. In their place, word processors, which automatically process and print text, electronic files in data banks (where words and numbers are stored as electronic digits) and data processing facilities (number crunching for statistical analysis) are being installed to create the so-called office of the future. The paper-pusher of the old-fashioned office is being replaced by a computer-wise knowledge worker in an electronic information network with automated clerical and administrative support services. It's happening now in trendsetting companies like Canadian Pacific Ltd., where such an automated information system has been in operation since 1980. Other trendsetters include Bell Northern Research, Shell Canada and Bell Canada.

As other companies run to match their productivity improvements or perish under competitive pressure, microchip technology is spreading as surely as the typewriter and telephone before it. Here's a brief account of a day in an intermediate job in the office of the future, based on the optimistic scenario described earlier but based in part on the automated system already in place in Canadian Pacific's headquarters in downtown Montreal and in its offices across Canada.

It's 9 A.M. and you've just sat down at your workstation, which differs from your old desk only by being plugged in. Through a desktop (or built-in) unit, which might combine a television-like screen with a retractable keyboard connected to a vast telecommunications network, you're all set to work. First, you "log" onto the system, by typing in your personal password, the equivalent of unlocking your office or desk, for an office is really an information system. Having entered the electronic information system, you begin your day by calling up your electronic calendar and those of other people in the company to which you have access — your subordinates, for instance. After checking what's on for the day, you call up your electronic "in" basket, containing documents sent from other departments or the word processing centre, plus telephone messages and electronic memos. Noticing one from your boss, who's noted a spare hour in your calendar and asked if you could meet with her, you deal with that first. On reading an electronic letter from someone in Germany who, along with you, is participating in a computer conference, you key in instructions to have it tucked into your electronic "computer conference" file on that subject.

With an hour to spare before your first meeting, you turn your television screen (a video display terminal or VDT) into an electronic workpad, keying in the code to extract from your electronic filing cabinet the report you've been preparing for an upcoming policy meeting. It's instantly displayed on the VDT screen. Through the communications systems at your fingertips, you gather up-to-the-minute sales data from regional offices, documented electronically when sales are made. You run these through some standard computer programs for statistical analysis to yield regional comparisons, combining the results with existing records to compare with market targets and trends. Then you devise the specifications for a graph that, drawn automatically, will highlight any trends or deviations most effectively. For further background information, you key or dial into the company's information services, first checking company records for any precedents on the type of suggestion you're about to make (more decentralized marketing, for instance), then dial outside the company into industry data banks your firm subscribes to and electronic newspaper files provided by InfoGlobe (*The Globe and Mail*) and *The New York Times*. Finally, you do a bit of computer modelling (simulated implementation of different variations on the policy you're suggesting) to demonstrate the possible effects of such a policy.

Beep-beep, your built-in electronic clock signals that your hour is up. You get up, grumbling about the archaic custom of going to meetings, but still going because there's no substituting for face-to-face brainstorming on the important stuff; besides, you're ready for a cup of coffee.

Such an office of the future is a giant step up from just automating individual job functions. Now these automated functions are integrated and set within a telecommunications network that lifts you, as on a winged chariot, from the print-bound information world of the past into the dynamic realm of electronic information. It's a world as vast as the communications networks (comprising telephones, telex, two-way television sets, cable and even the exotic satellites and optical fibres) and as powerful as the computer tools (word processors and other microcomputers, plus the larger mainframes), with automated clerical functions at your disposal.

The wonder of this new technology won't in itself cause companies to install it. They'll be pushed forward by the greater competitiveness the technology confers on the corporate opposition, forcing all companies to become more productive.

In fact, productivity pressure began building through the 1970s, against the backdrop of automation-triggered productivity gains in secondary manufacturing. In the late 1970s, an American business consulting firm reported that office operating costs had doubled over the previous decade, to half of total operating costs. Office productivity, however, had risen a scant 4 percent, compared with the impressive 80 percent productivity gains recorded in manufacturing after major investments in automation and increased mechanization (which tends to precede automation). This investment had left the average factory worker supported by $25,000 in capital equipment, while the office worker averaged a meagre $2,000 in little more than typewriters and dictaphones, both antique technologies.

Subsequent studies unmasked the monster of rising office costs and detailed the savings possible through electronic office systems. A 1980 report estimated that office wages and benefits were rising at 10 to 15 percent a year and that in banks and insurance companies, office labour costs accounted for 90 percent of total business costs.

Another study noted that the office's raw material, paper, rose in price by nearly 90 percent between 1973 and 1979 alone. And other research indicated that the cost of producing the traditional business letter had risen to between five and eight dollars by 1980. By comparison, it was estimated in a 1981 study that at the rate electronic communications costs were falling, it would cost less by 1983 to send a letter of seventy-five words by electronic mail than through the postal service, first class.

A Canadian company preparing for office automation identified a number of significant potential savings in preliminary feasibility study work. For instance, it was found that 70 percent of the outgoing mail was destined for elsewhere within the corporate network and, further, that copies of original correspondence represented over a third of that total. They also found that 55 percent of incoming mail originated within the corporate network. Together, these statistics showed enormous potential for savings in paper, postage and time through the use of electronic mail.

Exploring the potential for electronic filing, the office-of-the-future planners found 53 million sheets of paper on file, with the total increasing at 2.5 percent a year, since the pace of purging redundancy consistently lagged behind that of fresh input. Under a system of central data banks, only one copy of information would need to be kept, in electronic (digitized) form for automatic filing and retrieval. The savings would total 104,000 filing person-hours (or about fifty jobs' worth) and an estimated $250,000 in filing costs per year.

As compellingly as these studies argued for office automation, they couldn't effect its implementation overnight. Just as the availability of coal and the mechanization of work processes were preconditions to industrialization, certain preliminaries must precede automation, whether in an office, factory, forestry mill or farm. First, the work process must have been organized into a set of standard procedures or routines. This organizational process is generally referred to as scientific management. Its first step is the separation of the initiative phase from the execution phase of work. The execution function is then subdivided into component step-tasks, and standardized into a set routine.

Second, the equipment used must perform fixed routines, such as printing, adding or weaving. Such equipment will have some kind of control mechanisms, either mechanical cogs or electrical switches, that serve the same function as the punched cards in the Jacquard loom, namely, keeping the process in proper sequence.

Finally, there must be a wide assortment of electrical equipment already in place, particularly information-handling equipment. An office already extensively wired for electricity and with telephones and electric typewriters on every desk would be a much more likely candidate for office automation than one with manual typewriters and only one telephone in the outer office. Furthermore, if the office has been reorganized strictly by function, with typing pools handling most of the correspondence and standard forms and form letters used extensively, introducing office automation would offer immediate payoffs.

Once a company has installed the wiring necessary for data processing terminals, telephones and electric typewriters, plugging in word processing terminals is a small additional investment. Integrating word and data processing and adding graphics programs are further incremental investments adding ever increasing capability to the system. Putting terminals on the desks of professionals and managers, once the system has been extended up to their doors, is likewise a small additional investment yielding compounding benefits. The momentum builds once enough functions have been automated to justify integrating these into automated information systems. These then become available as professional and decisionmaking aids to an ever larger group of professionals and managers, with ever increasing benefits for ever smaller units of investment.

The spread of computer technology seems to involve three phases: the automation phase, where individual functions and procedures are automated; an integration phase, where the automated functions are woven into a computer communications network called an automated information system or a management information system; and an innovation stage, in which these integrated systems are applied as computer aids toward the creation of new economic activity and possibly new employment opportunities as well.

While the focus of the automation phase is on replacing mechanical activities with automated ones (for instance, replacing typing with word processing and filing with electronic files), the focus in the integration phase seems to be more on increasing the effectiveness of individuals who are expected to use the technology, not be replaced by it. By implying enhanced and expanded activity, this shift in focus seems conducive to unlocking the third, innovative phase in the implementation of computer technology. However, the actual flowering of the third phase seems also to depend on a positive shift in the user's attitude. This shift had not been apparent among trendsetters in office automation studies in the early 1980s; depressed economic conditions and high interest rates are only likely to discourage it further.

No matter how complex the information systems (also called computer communications or informatics systems) become, they can all be broken down into the five component parts found in the analytical engine conceived by Charles Babbage in the nineteenth century: an input and an output device (such devices, often called peripherals on word processing equipment, are the eyes, ears, hands and mouth of electronic information systems), a processing unit, a storage mechanism and a communicating unit. By looking at each component in turn, we can get an idea of the potential of the new technology for changing the face of work in offices.

Input

An input device can be as simple as a typewriter keyboard or as exotic as a light pen, which "writes" on the surface of the visual display screen to indicate, say, the outlines of a graph. Other exotic devices include the optical character reader incorporated in an office workstation or a supermarket checkout counter, and the "wand" whose beam of light reads the information contained in bar codes, postal codes or specially encoded cheques. These devices free clerical workers from manually keypunching or typing into a computer or word processing terminal often tedious volumes of boring information. The input unit digitizes the information entering as words, numbers or bar codes. Once the information has been reduced to data, it can then be processed, moved and stored automatically.

To take an example from outside the office setting, the most infamous input system in Canada is Canada Post's postal-code reader, which causes a fluorescent bar code to be sprayed onto an envelope. This allows mail to be automatically processed by the mail-sorting machines. The combination of the codes, optical character reader and processing unit has effectively stripped the skill and knowledge associated with routing mail away from the mail-sorting clerks and placed them in the machines. The mail sorter now serves the automated system; interestingly, the machines reject up to 40 percent of the mail, which then has to be processed by hand. Nevertheless, the deskilling associated with the automated system and the alleged machines-over-people manner of its implementation are considered key factors in the legendary militance of the inside postal workers.

Output

The output unit of a computer is the device that displays or records the data or information the computer has transmitted. (The data itself is also called output.) In a word processing unit, the output device is a video display terminal (VDT) or a printer for hard copies. Intelligent copiers (which produce photocopies automatically) and facsimile machines (which handle information originating in print form) are other output devices.

The computer-activated laser printer is an output device that demonstrates the power behind the new office technology. Operating at a maximum speed of 20,000 lines per minute, it could churn out one set of the entire annual output of Canadian books in less than an eight-hour day. It could also be turned on and instructed to typeset automatically from anywhere in the country. Many possible job losses can be identified here: not only through the automation of whole functions such as typesetting; but also in printing, because of the increased speed and the centralization laser printers offer and indirectly, because the amount of material distributed as inside corporate mail and through the post office would decrease.

In one application of an output device, a project code-named OASIS is designed to bring the office of the future to the House of Commons in Ottawa. Thanks to OASIS, notices of meetings of parliamentary committees will be printed out or displayed on the VDT screens to be installed in the offices of members of Parliament. Under the existing system, it costs an estimated four dollars per copy to have notices printed in a central location, then hand-delivered to MPs' offices. OASIS won't leave much work for Commons messengers; yet they weren't consulted in its design. Ironically, also, an interdepartmental user committee set up to help coordinate the introduction of office automation systems through the federal bureacracy has no representative of the unionized clerical and other public-service workers who will be using the new equipment or will be replaced by it.

Processing

The processing unit is the centre of any computer communications system and the seat of its power to automate. The smallest form of this unit is the microprocessor. Transforming a typewriter into an automatic word processor, the microprocessor allows the typist to shift paragraphs around and to store material for printing automatically. A job threat to typists can be identified. Just as the automated optical character reader automates the documentation or input function, the processing unit automates retyping, which traditionally occupies up to 70 percent of a typist's time. In old-fashioned unstructured offices, however, this didn't lead to job losses because typing was integrated with other job functions and occupied no more than 25 percent of a secretary's time. It required a reorganization along strictly job-function lines — with some people spending their entire day operating word processors, for instance — for the savings to become significant. In one word processing pool described in a 1981 study of automation in Ontario municipal government offices, word processor operators were able to average ten pages an hour, while regular typists, juggling typing with other responsibilities, averaged only two pages.

As well, the automatic storage and print features have made possible the storage of "boilerplate" form letters and paragraphs and the retention of addresses and whole mailing lists, which can be automatically printed on command. On the one hand, the almost completely automated letter allowed and encouraged more information work: the so-called personalized form letter. On the other hand, this additional activity can rarely create jobs because of the extensive automation involved. An office worker issuing new price lists to clients, for instance, merely calls up stored standard paragraphs on the subject, inserts the relevant new pricing information, types in the code for the mailing list of clients to which the notice is to be sent and, seconds or minutes later, the whole job, not just component functions of it, is complete. In Britain, studies of word processing installations in large insurance companies and government offices have documented productivity gains of nearly 200 percent. Workloads have been substantially increased, with either no increase in staff or some reductions when job vacancies are left unfilled.

In more sophisticated word processing systems, processing capabilities have been extended to include checking text for syntax and spelling (according to a built-in lexicon) and even having it typeset automatically. While both these innovations automate "people" functions, the effect on typesetters is particularly worrisome, because this craft has already been whittled down by technological changes. Photocomposition swept through the printing trade in the 1970s, eliminating the skill of setting blocks of type, and leaving only the layout and "keying" aspects of the process. (And although it never earned the secretaries "craft" status, the skill of setting up the format of reports and documents is likewise being taken from clerical workers and incorporated into word processors.)

In offices that have intelligent copiers, printing instructions (say, six copies, printed both sides) can be encoded in the text at the word processing stage, and the whole package can be beamed electronically down the hall to the copier. While photocopying is certainly not an enriching experience, turning it over to machines eliminates one more facet from multifunction jobs and makes it easier to streamline work activities into, for instance, word processing pools.

Finally, the processing unit inside the computer terminal might go into action when programmed by a set of instructions sent electronically from another city. The processing could conclude with the results automatically sent back to the word processor or computer terminal that initiated the work. In this case, the two terminals would be "talking" to each other, eliminating the need for two people to be in touch with each other, but eliminating social contact as well.

Storage

The next component of office information systems is the storage or memory mechanism, the electronic equivalent of a filing cabinet and library. Technically, storage can take a number of forms, with the per-unit storage cost depending on how quickly one can get at specific information. So-called "smart" word processors have their own memory microchips, allowing a limited amount of information to be held "on-line" within them; this is the most expensive form of filing. If the information isn't to be reused immediately, it can be stored at lower cost on floppy disks, which usually have "random access" memory. This allows instant retrieval of specific information stored anywhere on them. Magnetic tape reels are a cheaper form of storage; however, their sequential retrieval mechanism requires the user to run through the entire information file to reach the specific information needed. In whatever form, electronic information storage automates both filing and file retrieval functions, two of the most boring tasks in the office but also time-consuming sources of employment.

Communications

The communications component weaves all the others together into the integrated office-of-the-future system, also called the intelligence universe. In offices, it links word processors to make them *communicating* word processors. It connects word processors to intelligent copiers, computer terminals and outside data banks.

Communications media can take many forms, including standard telephone lines, the more powerful two-way (coaxial) cables and fibre optics, which have a still greater capacity. A single cable containing twelve glass fibres can carry more than 200 television channels. The actual link between communications media is made by a modem (*modulator-demodulator*), a device that converts acoustic signals to electrical signals and vice versa. In addition to the transmission component, communications also involves switching mechanisms, which route messages through the maze of transmission lines and different communications systems to reach their final destinations. One form of switching mechanism is the private-branch exchange, which is an automated version of the old-fashioned telephone switchboard. The newest versions of these exchanges can handle data processing as well as voice.

The communications component makes possible endless combinations of component parts in the electronic Meccano set that is the office of the future. For example, consider the following three variations of word processing systems. A stand-alone word processing system is, as the name implies, largely self-contained, with no real communications component. It prints out what is keyed or otherwise put into it. Such a system would likely be found in small businesses. By comparison, in a shared-logic system, several word processors are hooked up to one computer processing unit. The benefit is in the lower costs and central control over the processing of information. The disadvantage to the office workers is in having to work on a terminal that is essentially "dumb" — because of the employer's attitude to using the technology. With all the processing intelligence locked in the central unit, they can do nothing more than put information into the system and complete work according to instructions relayed from the central unit.

In the third arrangement, called distributed-logic systems, word processors have some built-in processing capability (for instance, automated typesetting and graph design) and are also able to communicate with other word processors and to tap into the central processing unit (possibly a large mainframe computer) where major data processing jobs can be done. This setup allows for the savings of centralization as well as local autonomy, diversity and the potential for job growth.

So it's not the technology itself but how it's applied that most influences the employment outcome of office automation. The person working on the intelligent terminal in the distributed-logic system has at least the potential to apply the automated information systems as tools and take on more enriched job functions (preparing graphs, for instance) as the traditional ones (retyping, filing, making copies) are automated. But the work of the person working at a dumb terminal is whittled down from several job functions to only one — a form of deskilling in its own right — with no opportunity for the worker to take on or learn new tasks. Cut off from the wider scope of things, such operators can end up feeling that their work has no meaning. As well, the isolating and alienating effect is compounded by the reduction of wages in such jobs to a piecework basis and by the measurement of performance by monitoring operators' keystrokes per hour. As we'll see later on, this tendency to restrict a person's activity to one isolated task can result in mental distress.

Yet the dumb terminal setup is a common feature of office automation systems, particularly in large corporate and government offices. One can understand the attraction for the person wanting to guarantee his return through maximum use of the word processing equipment, which, after all, costs ten times more than an electric typewriter. Looking strictly at traditional information-handling needs of a typical large corporation, the centralized word processing pool featuring a cluster of essentially dumb terminals linked to a central processing unit makes good economic sense. Taking a larger and longer-term perspective, however, a company that allowed word processor operators to remain integrated within the larger office setting, to keep up with new developments and related operating needs, might find itself less dependent on hiring new skilled workers to help launch these developments. The existing staff could acquire the new knowledge and skills through on-the-job learning experiences.

The $150-Billion Business

Not surprisingly, the five components of office information systems correspond to the major industry groups fighting for dominance in the lucrative new business of selling office-of-the-future equipment and systems services. Industry magazines estimated North American revenues of $150 billion a year beginning in 1982.

The war for dominance will be won by whichever company or industry group can successfully install its line of equipment (input, output, processing, storage, communications) at the hub of the office's activity. Each group is busily adding variations of the others' equipment to its product line. Office equipment companies, which first introduced the intelligent typewriter with floppy disk information storage, see the text processing and storage unit as the central feature, with communications, computing, printing and graphics as support systems only. The computer companies, of course, describe word processing as an extension of data processing, and offer text creating, editing, storing and retrieving as programmable features of their central or distributed computer systems. The telephone companies and others in the telecommunications business present themselves as the traffic cops directing the information content of the office through their switching units and vast communications networks. Northern Telecom's Displayphone, scheduled to hit the market in 1982, integrates the familiar telephone handset with a retractable typewriter-style keyboard and a display screen for digitized voice messages and information, called up from data banks via a keypad, familiar from push-button phones. Linked to a printer and boasting graphics capability in its software, it can produce documents and handle electronic mail as well. Bell Canada began offering a store-and-forward electronic messaging service in 1981.

Among other companies fighting for a respectable presence in the office of the future, if not for control over it, are those specializing in graphics, offering decisionmaking support systems based on the importance they feel graphs and other visual techniques represent in the business of management and corporate communications. Companies such as Xerox that entered offices selling copying machines are incorporating optical scanner devices and high-speed printing mechanisms into their machines. They are integrating these into a single word processing, data processing, filing and copying network, and even, in Xerox's case, selling network-building (it's called Ethernet) as a new service. Filing cabinet manufacturers are marketing filing systems called computer-assisted retrieval systems. And on the fringes, there are companies selling gadgets that can sometimes break logjams of cost or institutional resistance by the sheer playfulness and seeming inconsequence of their innovations. Electronic watches have now evolved to include wrist-mounted calculators. They could soon incorporate a Dick Tracy-style message unit several times more sophisticated than the pocket beepers used by doctors and travelling salespeople. A Montreal-based company sells car-based telephone systems, while Toronto-based National Electronic Industries has launched a cordless telephone. A company called the New Ventures Group is selling a Voice Message System (VMS), which is simply mounted on existing phones. It can send, receive, store or broadcast voice messages to any other user of the system twenty-four hours a day, anywhere in the world.

An Office of the Future

Having explored the component parts, it's time to put the office of the future back together, by returning to a company typical of those with a state-of-the-art office, namely Canadian Pacific. When this Montreal-based corporation launched its own version of the office of the future, it looked beyond using word processing as a better means of producing reports and other information. It rethought its entire approach to information. The result was not unrelated to the fact that the principal architects on the interdepartmental committee were not the traditional office workers who saw information as an end in itself, but the new information workers associated with computers. They approached information from a process or systems point of view, seeing it as a means to an end — that end being decisionmaking. The difference would result in their office of the future employing more *knowledge* workers (professionals applying information) rather than strictly *information* workers (people handling, processing or producing information).

The distinction is vital. Most traditional office workers are not knowledge but information workers: they document, record and process information, file, store and distribute it. In short, they do what the component features of automated information systems now offer to do automatically. In Canadian Pacific's office of the future, this work *is* being done automatically.

The most significant innovation in the total information systems approach is not in automating the component functions of information production, but in actually eliminating (by superseding) much of the information production that clerical workers do, supervisors oversee and administrators organize. Maintaining records and reporting are becoming largely redundant because these activities are being replaced by general-purpose computer programs and automated functions. For example, when a railway clerk in Regina types in the details on some merchandise to be shipped on CP Rail, the waybill information becomes an instant part of any freight movement report someone might generate anywhere in Canadian Pacific's electronic information system (Vancouver, Montreal or Regina) through a few keyword instructions typed into the computer terminal on his or her desk. These keyword instructions might call for the data to be arranged or processed according to cargo category or destination or in relation to the previous month's figures and projected totals. All the work, including the percentage distributions and comparisons, would be generated automatically. No more does the decisionmaker depend on some report writer; nor does she depend on a supervisor having sent the preliminary reports in on time, or on an administrator having designed effective reporting procedures, or on support staff having followed them. Yet these occupations — supervision, administration and clerical work — accounted for much of the office employment growth over the past thirty years.

In the automation of the 1950s and 1960s, Canadian Pacific's computer staff confined their efforts to major statistical projects, such as accounting, payroll and freight data. The increasing proliferation and sophistication of analyzing routines — daily revenue by region and commodity group, compared to previous years' trends and so on — greatly enhanced management's effectiveness but didn't much affect the traditional information workers involved in filing, retyping and recordkeeping. But gradually the computer people extended their activities, using the microchip to automate more and more of these traditional office functions. This represented the first phase of the computerization process, the automation of individual functions.

In the second, integration phase, VDTs are being installed on the desktops of managers throughout the corporation, with each terminal hooked into the company's electronic information system and into each other, via dedicated phone lines — lines that have been set aside exclusively for one customer. In creating this integrated on-line information network, CP is not only increasing the effectiveness of decisionmakers; it is greatly extending the scope for automation as well. For instance, in the automation of waybill preparation, the shipping clerk merely types into the computer keyboard the pattern number, weight and car number of the merchandise being shipped. The taxing work of calculating freight charges and the tedious work of correctly completing the shipping forms is now all done automatically. Car movements are also monitored automatically.

At head office, the integrated computer communications system includes the following features: electronic filing, mail, messaging (and, to a certain extent, daily scheduling), text editing, word and data processing, remote computing and access to data banks both within and outside the company. Most of these features are automated clerical and administrative functions that professionals and managers now activate on a self-serve basis. A year after the system was introduced to the Information Systems department (before the second wave of automation, it was called the Data Systems department; the change is a significant reflection of its wider scope), all fifty of the senior professional–managerial group were using their desktop terminals to send and receive up to 75 percent of what secretaries used to handle in print form. As one example, two executives (both happened to be in Montreal, but they could have easily been in separate cities, and located at home instead of the office) used their terminals to confer on the drafting of a policy document, exchanging drafts six times before agreeing on the final version, which was then checked for spelling by a secretary and printed automatically. The executives had not only saved the time and cost of having six drafts typed, retyped, copied and sent by messenger; they also avoided having to hold a meeting.

Now the company, which was founded in 1881 as a transportation service supported by communications and evolved into a communications service supported by information, is selling the software "blueprints" for this office-of-the-future system. They consist of operating programs for the system's various features.

Despite its enlarged activities, the Information Systems department actually shrank in size, and beneath the surface, the composition of its staff has changed dramatically. Between 1972 and 1980, the number of clerical workers dropped by 130, while employment in the professional–managerial group rose by 110, with the proportion of clerical workers dropping from 80 to 45 percent. There are three employment effects here. First, there is the obvious shortfall between the jobs lost at the bottom and those added at the top. Second, there appears to be a skills gap: only two of the 130 displaced clerical workers moved up to the professional–managerial ranks, which were filled mainly from outside the company. Of the others, some left the company and the rest were given lateral transfers to departments as yet unautomated.

In the Human Resources (personnel) department of the same company, nearly all professional, executive-level vacancies between 1975 and 1981 had been filled from outside the company, by professionals who would be able to exploit features of the computer communications systems — computer modelling, for instance — for sophisticated analysis. The personnel who used to rise from the clerical and line operations ranks through supervisory and administrative positions to the top spots are left behind as the new professionals extend the standards of performance by their computer-aided work. Subtly, these traditional middle managers are downgraded as well. The skills and knowledge they've mastered to become supervisors and administrators are absorbed into the computer communications systems as automated processes and procedures; as well, computerized instruction and automatic forwarding of work automate whole functions associated with supervisory work. This development is particularly significant for women, who have only recently gained access to these traditional administrative and supervisory jobs as a stepping stone out of the clerical ranks.

Jobless economic growth was the third, less readily detected development. As the name change from data processing to information systems suggested, the department greatly expanded its sphere of activity to take in administrative-service work which in a paper-based office milieu had gone on in other departments.

While CP is a trendsetter in exploiting the new technology, it's certainly not alone. A 1981 federal government study on computers and jobs found employment shifts even more pronounced than CP's at the University of Calgary's Information Systems department. Whereas there was a fairly even split between managerial and professional workers and operations and support workers in 1968, the support group's share of employment had dropped by just over 20 percent by 1981. Adding fuel to the concern of jobless economic growth, the study noted that while the workload had more than doubled between 1973 and 1981, overall employment had only increased by 16 percent. Not surprisingly, more than half the women were concentrated in the support-level clerical positions, compared with a fifth of the men.

A 1981 study of computer communications in Ontario municipal government offices contains similar revelations. After automated tax billing and payment processing was introduced in Oshawa, Ontario, twelve people could look after 40,000 properties, where previously it had taken sixteen people to administer 23,000 properties. Three of the four displaced clerical workers retired during the transition period and their jobs were simply left unfilled. The other worker was given a lateral transfer. In their place, the city hired two professionals, an analyst and a programmer.

At Toronto City Hall, where up to 80 percent of all financial transactions were computerized by 1981, the technology allowed more information to be handled while employment levels rose only marginally and job qualifications went up. In 1970, for instance, finance department clerks required only high school education. By 1980, postsecondary training and education was becoming a more prevalent requirement.

The addition of automated typesetting and printing to the word-processing capabilities also led to indirect job losses. The city hired four extra people with various computer skills, only partly to look after the automated typesetting and printing of City Council minutes. But at the commercial printer that had previously printed the minutes, enough work for eight jobs was lost.

Reviewing the record of computerization in the office, it's possible to identify three general trends. Traditional clerical jobs seem to be disappearing as automated clerical and administrative support services become more common. But the extent of the change isn't as clear as it would be if there were mass layoffs of secretaries. Job vacancies are being left unfilled, and clerical jobs are being replaced by professional and managerial jobs. As well, information-handling workloads are being greatly increased with no additions in staff, highlighting the jobless economic growth phenomenon which stifles employment even if it doesn't produce layoffs. The cumulative effect is dramatic. Clerical employment growth has slowed almost to a halt. In public administration, clerical employment grew by less than 1 percent between 1975 and 1980, while managerial employment jumped 22 percent. As well, many of the new jobs that *are* being created are part-time positions, effectively masking reduced workloads; 30 percent of new jobs created between 1975 and 1980 were part-time jobs, often involving fewer than twenty hours a week. Statistics Canada also found that in the 1975–1980 period, more women were accepting part-time jobs because they were unable to find full-time employment. As well, full-time employees are being replaced by part-time workers, further concealing the decreased workloads.

These developments are especially worrisome for working

35

women, 35 percent of whom depend on clerical positions for employment. Furthermore, the number of women in the work force is expected to increase dramatically over the next decade, at roughly the same rate at which clerical employment opportunities had been growing through the 1960s and early 1970s. Patterns of socialization, reinforced by structures and employment patterns in the workplace, suggest that women won't easily stop orienting themselves to clerical employment and being relegated to clerical job areas; yet the prospects for employment there are fast diminishing.

Aside from the quantity of jobs, the new technology also seems to be reducing the quality of work available. Multifunction jobs as secretaries, for instance, are being replaced by single-function jobs as word processor operators where the restricted scope of activity and skills further hampers the clerical worker's ability to move into other areas of work. This subtle deskilling widens the gap of qualifications between clerical and other types of work.

In a second overall trend, office work is becoming more professional, and existing professional work is becoming more demanding. It's being intensified not only through the automation of the routine clerical tasks that professionals traditionally did themselves, but also through the implied necessity of doing more sophisticated research, analysis and decisionmaking using the automated information systems and computer power now at their disposal. Again, this has implications for women, who are underrepresented in the office-related professions — such as accounting — and who now must make an even larger leap in education and skills (including computer skills) in order to enter these lines of work.

The third trend is that office administration and management is being transformed. As traditional reporting is automated, reducing the need to create and manage reporting hierarchies, and as computer monitoring and other developments erode traditional supervisory work, middle management is itself becoming more professional. In some offices, the good all-round manager is being replaced by a specialist resource person, often with computer skills: the manager of data communications systems, the systems designer, the manager of applications programming or of data banks.

36

Here again, the implications for women are discouraging. In the automation of traditional middle-management work, they are losing what little ground for career mobility they have won in recent years, and they are under-represented in the ranks of the new computer specialists.

Oops, a little malfunction in the computer. For a moment there you were worth a fortune.

3

Automation
in Service Industries

The microprocessor had been around for barely five years when its effect on service-sector jobs sparked a flurry of study and concerned discussion. A German study, the Siemens report, estimated that 40 percent of white-collar workers could lose their jobs through automation. The Nora Minc report commissioned by the French government estimated that 30 percent of bank and insurance workers could be displaced by automation in information work. An international study published by a British-based consulting group predicted 15 to 20 percent job reduction in the hotel business, and within the telephone business, 25 percent job cuts in handling long-distance calls and 50 percent in manufacturing equipment. Other studies in the 1970s produced similarly dire prognoses.

The predictions for job losses in these industries struck a chord of fear, because this sector accounted for most of the jobs created in the postwar era. In the 1970s alone, service industries accounted for 80 percent of the new jobs. By the late 1970s, though, that growth was levelling off sharply, and no new sector was emerging to replace it as a source of large-scale low-skilled employment.

Banks, insurance companies, the retail trade, government and public corporations were pillars of this emerging sector. Their growth stemmed from a number of factors, including greater affluence and the growth of the public sector. The technology itself was a third factor; there's no doubt that the computer's tremendous capacity to process data helped the sector to grow, at least for a time, since it increased the amount of information that could be handled as well as the scope for applying information.

The service-sector growth also coincided with the expanding role of women in the work force. During the 1970s alone, the number of working women increased by 62 percent. Furthermore, a similar increase is expected during the 1980s, adding an additional 1.8 million women to the job market, and raising women's rate of participation in the work world from roughly 50 percent in 1980 to something close to the 70 percent range that has been achieved in Sweden and other Western European countries.

Given the coincidence of these two developments in the employment scene, it isn't surprising that most women (80 percent in 1980) work in service industries. Most are also found within a narrow range of clerical, sales and service occupations that have traditionally featured both low qualifications and low wages.

The banks illustrate clearly the developments in the female labour force. During the 1960s and 1970s, the banks were among the most dependable employers of women, hiring at a rate slightly ahead even of the rapid entry of women into the labour force, for a total in 1980 that was 300 percent higher than their female employment in 1950. In 1980, women represented 70 percent of total bank employment of 151,000; 80 percent of the women were concentrated in clerical positions.

Some of the jobs held most often by women include bank tellers, telephone operators, typists, cashiers and retail clerks. They're called female job ghettos because they're almost exclusively held by women, because of their low-wage status and because there are almost no opportunities to move out of these jobs into the more demanding and better-paid professional and managerial occupations.

The jobs share one other feature as well: by and large they can all be classed as support work, as opposed to work that involves exercising control and initiative — making decisions, for instance. In the office setting, the support work is clerical and administrative support. Throughout the service sector, the support work involves delivering services — tellers delivering banking services, for example, and telephone operators, long-distance service — or administering retail sales, as cashiers and stock clerks do. Broadly speaking, the two-thirds of the female labour force employed in clerical, sales and service occupations are involved in such support-type work. That work is now being extensively automated. Furthermore, the preconditions for automation are in most cases already in place — standardized work, mechanical processes and a control function.

As microchip-based automation sweeps through the service sector, research reports seem to agree that women will be "hardest hit," as one put it. Not only are women trapped by the no-exit characteristics of the female job ghettos but, even more importantly, they are confined by the entrenched attitudes that created those ghettos in the first place — namely, that "women's work" is by definition support work. Such work is consistent with their status as wives and mothers, which women tend to consider, consciously or not, their primary roles in life.

Research has found that not only do women see the wife-and-mother role as their primary goal in life but they also regard working outside the home as a secondary, fringe activity. Hence, it's been found, they avoid taking the tough career-preparation courses such as enriched math in high school and college. Armed with few practical skills and often unfocussed knowledge when they enter the job market, they readily accept being relegated to the fringes of employment — the female job ghettos and the part-time work force of which they form 75 percent.

Automation in the service sector, then, is occurring against the backdrop of women's precarious status in and, at the same time, increasing dependence on, the jobs within it. It's also set against an economic backdrop starkly different from the expansionary 1960s, that seemed such absolute proof of the assertion that the rise in productivity from automation spurs further economic growth and increased employment.

History has shown that the rise of the service sector was as much a result of other factors as of technology's productivity quotient, and that the skill requirements of emerging service-industry jobs were felicitously low, so the people being displaced from processing industries through automation could move into them — driving trucks, providing security and other services — without special training. Some examples of current automation in the service sector will also demonstrate that increased economic activity isn't necessarily accompanied by increased employment. The focus or governing purpose has to change in the transition through the automation and integration phases into the innovation phase.

Banks

The banks are typical of service-sector growth and of the role computers have played in that growth. Not only were banks expanding (from about five thousand branches in 1960 to some seventy-five hundred by 1980), but computers allowed them to handle vastly larger volumes of information ($108 billion in deposits in 1979, for instance, compared with $13 billion in 1960). As well, when they introduced data processing to their operations in the 1960s and early 1970s, there was an initial overlap between the electronic information workers and those working in print. Records of daily bank transactions were at first transported to the banks' computer centre, where keypunch operators laboriously transcribed the information into digital code for the computer. Later data-entry clerks supplanted keypunch operators and transaction data was communicated through batch processing, but a lot of overlap remained. This was not noticed, however, in the atmosphere of economic optimism that had carried over from the 1960s. With the second wave of automation made possible by the microprocessor, however, computer technology spread out to even the smallest branch and the overlap disappeared.

Just as the direction of change has been the same in banks as in a traditional office setting, the motivation for change has been similar as well: the proliferation of paperwork and related costs.

The preconditions for automation — which are the same throughout the service sector — are similar as well. Assiduous scientific management has standardized much of banking work into set routines and job functions; control was lodged in the fixed routines, procedures and accompanying forms; and mechanical equipment was being replaced by electric and electronic equipment.

Three examples will illustrate the extent of automation in banks. Optical character readers and automated processing units (often minicomputers) in regional centres have enabled twenty-four-hour cheque handling through automated cheque processing. The technique is similar to automated mail sorting in post offices, although this system can do much more. Whereas previously the cheque itself had to be sent from place to place, now only the relevant electronic information is sent — at a cost estimated at 20 percent of the paper cheque's cost. Once the information has been digitized, it can then be automatically transmitted to balance accounts and be processed in innumerable ways — to calculate interest and service charges and to update files for recordkeeping and management analysis, to name a few.

At the second, integration phase, computer terminals were installed directly in bank branches to enable on-line data processing. Previously, a bank teller had to prepare reports on all the financial transactions handled each day. Once the reports were checked by a supervisor, they were forwarded to the computer centre, where a data-entry clerk (originally a keypunch operator) fed the information into the computer system. With the on-line integration development, however, the teller can enter the data directly into the computer at the branch terminal, thereby bypassing the data-entry clerk. Furthermore, this is not done separately, but happens simultaneously as the teller keys the transaction data into the terminal to expedite the banking service for the customer.

Several sources of job loss could be identified: condensing what had been two separate job functions — documenting and recording transactions — into one; consolidating the tasks of several people — the teller, the supervisor and the data-entry clerk — into tasks for one person; and outright automation of component functions of delivering bank services, such as automated update on the bank's electronic files and automated printout or output of transaction data into the customer's passbook.

With the introduction of automated tellers or banking machines, starting in the late 1970s, another potential source of job loss became apparent. Now customers themselves key in the transaction information, which is automatically processed and recorded both in the bank's computer centre and the customer's bankbook. Just as automated clerical functions are handed over to the professionals in the office of the future as self-serve automated information activities, so basic banking is being handed over to the consumer as a self-serve activity. This development provides a good example of the simplification and deskilling of clerical work. If the unschooled consumer can do the work, it *must* be simple.

The automated teller machine or ATM consists of a microcomputer terminal mounted in the wall of a bank or shopping mall (and, potentially at least, at factories and offices), capable of processing a limited set of transactions. In Royal Bank terminals, these are deposits, withdrawals, transfers from one account to another, and payment of utility and credit-card bills. These are the core of bank services, accounting for some 80 percent of traditional bank business.

The ATM input unit is a combination of a keyboard connected on-line to the bank's computer, an optical scanner unit and a special "membership" card. This card, also called a personal-access or personal-identity card, has a magnetic code strip that is read by the optical scanner unit inside the terminal. This code and the personal security code that the customer keys in at the keyboard allow the customer to enter the bank's now completely integrated computer communications network.

By 1981, Continental Bank in the United States had nearly a million customers using more than five hundred terminals. In Britain, more than two thousand terminals were in use. In Canada, the Royal Bank, the Bank of Montreal and the Toronto Dominion Bank had close to fifty terminals each in Toronto alone.

As the automated bank functions, now integrated into financial information systems, also become available to the administrative and professional staff as computer aids, the focus seems to shift away from strictly labour savings toward working more effectively. Accounts managers can keep a closer eye on reserves and overall cash flow through instant access to the up-to-the-minute data banks and analysis routines developed by computer software specialists (who write and design computer logic routines, or programs). Computer-aided loans processing allows the loans officer to handle a much higher workload. The clerical form-filling work is stripped away and largely automated, and the analysis-of-risk arithmetic is handled by a computer-model program once the variable data (collateral, pay-back period and so on) has been keyed into the appropriate formulas.

It's hard to say whether such computer aids truly enhance what these professionals do. They could merely intensify the work by whittling away all but the most difficult work of actually judging the risk-worthiness of a loan applicant, while widening the skills gap between this professional position and the clerical ranks. The routine analysis and form-preparation work could conceivably have served as stepping-stone training ground for a bank worker moving out of the clerical ranks.

The suggestion of deskilling is borne out in another, similar example: processing letters of credit. The Continental Bank in the United States, after first standardizing the work into a series of routine task-functions, automated the entire series. Clerical staff and paraprofessionals involved in this work were first asked to explain exactly how they judged the credit-worthiness of customers. Judgment was reduced to logic, and these logical deductions were translated into a computer program. Now a clerical worker merely has to feed the raw data into the computer system for the credit-evaluation process to roll automatically. What formerly required more than thirty processing steps involving at least fourteen people acting on material in six different files now takes only one person at one computer terminal, connected on-line within the bank's computer communications system. The work also takes less than a day; it used to take at least three days.

The Royal Bank and the Bank of Montreal, at the forefront of banking automation in Canada, are extending their already impressive computer communications networks to include word and text processing. Continental Bank and Citibank in the United

States have already taken this step, with sophisticated word processing capability integrated with the network of interactive computers in the branches and bank headquarters. Over the course of this transition, Citibank is reported to have reduced its clerical, typing and secretarial staff by more than half, from 10,500 to 5,000.

Continental Bank has also pioneered in turning employees' homes into the equivalent of electronic cottages by installing computer or word processing terminals. Bank executives can activate the bank's central word processing pool by phoning in their dictation. Some dictation is routed to clerical workers equipped with terminals in their homes. The bank is actively promoting this home work, and it could become a major new development in employment; however, there are drawbacks such as the tendency toward isolation.

Whether they're enhancing bankers' work or not, computer aids are certainly allowing banks to expand their range of services, an example of the third phase —innovation — of the application of the technology. These new services include daily-interest savings accounts and multibranch banking. However, little additional personnel was required in launching these new services. Furthermore, the additional people were largely professionals in accounting and computer science, and they were needed only to design and implement the enabling computer communications systems. Once in place, the new services ran themselves; no clerical support staff were needed, because clerical support work was executed automatically. In fact the ATM represents a whole new concept in the service sector: a completely automated system for providing or delivering services, in this case, banking services. It's worth remembering that of the two-thirds of the Canadian labour force in the service sector, the majority work delivering services rather than creating or selling them.

In another example of self-service, some banks have developed semiautomated data analysis programs and made these available to corporate clients for their direct use. As an example, the computer terminal in a corporate client's office is connected on-line to the client's account files within the bank's information systems network. This not only saves a phone call from the client to the bank but it also allows the company accountant to bypass the bank's accounts-service personnel. In a reverse variation of this same theme, some banks offer budget-management computer aids and payroll-management services to corporate clients.

The suggestion of enlarged employment opportunities through new bank services is misleading, however; what seems to be extra work for a bank employee is actually an indirect centralization of clerical and administrative support work that had previously been done within the client companies. With the automation of the administrative and much of the clerical work, one can predict that the one bank clerical worker operating these service functions is doing the work that had required many more people with more knowledge and skills.

The 1981 Bank Act clipped the banks' wings somewhat by preventing them from providing such decidedly nonfinancial services as labour analysis and management report preparation; these services are now being offered by data processing and computer service bureaus. But there are other directions the banks can pursue in the creation of new services, such as personalized retirement savings plans and related financial counselling, for both individuals and corporate clients. The ATMs are but one vehicle for delivering these new information services. In the future, customers might receive them through home videotex systems or terminals in their offices. Soon, corporate client companies that have an on-line link to the bank's computer will be able to use desktop terminals in their corporate information network for basic banking as well.

Given the singular lack of employment growth in the innovation-phase services already implemented, though, one has to wonder how many new jobs will be created in these new frontiers of banking. If the focus in extending services is simply on cutting costs, the potential for new job growth might not extend beyond those few professionals who are needed to design and implement the new self-services. Shifting the focus toward creating and selling new bank services will probably have a lot to do with the prevailing economic climate, as well as employment policies on technological change.

If the banks aren't actually heralding jobless economic growth in Canadian service industries, they have certainly reversed their tradition of being major employers of clerical workers. Between

47

1975 and 1980, relative clerical employment in banks fell by 5 percent. Furthermore, while refusing to disclose employment statistics, two major banks acknowledged that they had substantially increased their hirings of part-time workers, from virtually none in the early 1970s to some 15 percent of staff less than a decade later.

This adds one more dimension to the vulnerability of the women who fill the great majority of bank clerical jobs. Not only do most lack union protection (fewer than a hundred of the 7,600 bank branches in Canada are unionized), they are held on the bare fringes of employment by their combined status as support staff, as denizens of job ghettos and as part-time workers. Part-time workers lack most of the job benefits, such as pensions, provided to full-time workers and are rarely considered for promotion. They are not taken seriously as members of an organization and tend to be regarded simply as a convenient reserve labour pool.

Insurance Companies

Like the banks, insurance companies in Canada have grown tremendously in employment and economic strength over the past thirty years, although job growth was only 14 percent during the 1970s compared with 20 percent during the 1960s. In 1980 insurance companies employed 62,000 Canadians. Like banks, insurance companies hire a lot of women and employ a lot of clerical workers; 70 percent of their women employees are in the clerical ranks.

Like the banks, insurance companies deal in information. In the form of insurance contracts and premiums, information constitutes some 90 percent of the work. Finally, like the banks, insurance companies are among the most advanced enterprises in the automation of their information work. At least one Canadian company has gone beyond the stage of merely automating individual information-handling job functions and even integrating automated functions to provide computer aids to its professional and managerial staff. It's poised on the brink of offering new services, such as personalized insurance at group insurance rates, with the innovations made possible by automated information systems.

In the first wave of automation, computer installations in insurance companies were confined to head offices and applications restricted to large data processing requirements for cost accounting and financial management. Branches maintained their own records and forwarded summary statistics for batch processing by the computer at head office. With the second wave of automation, the technology came out to the branches to automate not only recordkeeping but many other clerical functions as well. In head offices, word processing was added to the already extensive computer system to automate much of the work associated with issuing insurance policies. Computer programs developed for calculating premium payment schedules effectively automated the arithmetic and documentation aspects of issuing the policy. In other applications, the automation of premium billing and payment handling not only reduces documentation, mail handling and recordkeeping but also collapses what had been a series of tasks by a number of people in both the branch and the head office to what is, in most cases, one short human intervention. Premium notices are sent out automatically and are increasingly collected automatically as well, through electronic funds transfers. Now, with the increasing integration of electronic information files and automated procedures, birthdates in all policyholders' files are automatically monitored. The approach of a birthdate triggers the automatic production of a personalized letter promoting additional insurance coverage. This relieves the insurance sales agent of keeping track of policyholders' birthdays and represents an expansion of insurance service with no increase in jobs.

With the automation of clerical functions resulting in the computerization of whole insurance procedures, companies have integrated these procedures with the electronic data banks and computer processing prowess developed during the 1960s to develop computer aids for increasing numbers of professional and managerial staff.

A major Toronto-based insurance company — cited in *Women and the Chip*, a series of case studies on information automation (informatics) in Canadian service industries — is doing this in two stages. First it separated the analytical part of underwriting work from the essentially clerical part of translating the results of that analysis into the premium that an insurance policyholder must pay. This didn't result in increased clerical employment, since the clerical work associated with collecting client data, searching files and preparing the policy forms had already been largely automated. It did, though, reduce employment needs at the professional level. The company anticipated a major expansion of insurance business without having to hire additional underwriters; with the routine work removed, though, it also intensified underwriter work. The next step — automating risk evaluation — could intensify underwriting work even more. Here, the considerations affecting the risk factor of an individual are drawn from the company's and larger industry data banks, then electronically analyzed to yield a standard model for assessing risk in order to calculate premiums. Once the model has been developed, the underwriter will only tackle the most difficult cases, those that constitute exceptions to the rules. Increasingly, too, such developments mean that underwriters will have to work directly with computers, possibly designing and writing programs themselves.

At the level of middle management, it's hard to know whether this work is being eliminated or simply drastically transformed. Certainly traditional administrative and supervisory work — that stepping stone out of the clerical job ghetto — is being automated. Traditional supervisory work becomes redundant through computer monitoring. Increasingly, computer-aided instruction is taking over another major component of supervisory work as well. In the insurance company studied in *Women and the Chip*, the ratio of supervisor-instructors to staff was 1 to 15, compared with 1 to 5 before computer-aided instruction. The administration of reporting hierarchies and procedures, among other operating procedures, is eclipsed by automated information-handling and administrative support systems. The automation of whole operational processes, such as issuing premium notices and processing payments, and of entire administrative procedures, such as reporting and cash-flow management, effectively eliminates other administrative components of middle-management work. As well, all the skill and knowledge associated with drafting an operational budget or reporting procedures are absorbed into a computer program or model into which the relevant statistics and data merely

50

need to be slotted. If the position has not been automated as such, it has decidedly been deskilled to a clerical level. The office administrator could be replaced by a technical or professional resource person, able to work with computers and even design new computer aids. Such persons, at least during the transition to automated information systems, are not being drawn up from the clerical ranks. They are being hired from outside the company, and have university degrees in mathematics, computer science and engineering.

In a sense, this also illustrates the shift toward self-service in the service sector. Just as providing basic banking and insurance services is shifting from the hands of paid employees into the hands of unpaid consumers, so providing internal administrative and clerical services within these companies is being automated into a self-serve function in the hands of either the remaining clerical staff or the senior professional–managerial group.

So many of the changes are occurring beneath the surface, drastically altering the content of general middle- and senior-management jobs; yet some shifts are evident in total job figures. In the insurance company studied in *Women and the Chip*, total employment rose by 260 over the course of three years ending in mid-1980, with most of that concentrated in the specialist–professional ranks; clerical workers' share of total employment actually dropped by 12 percent. Furthermore, the skills difference between the two groups widened considerably, abetted by the sharp increase in external hirings to fill professional positions. Confirming the proportions of that difference, there was a high failure rate among the people who were promoted to professional–specialist ranks from within the company.

In another insurance company, included in a University of Calgary study on jobs and computers, business was expanded considerably without significant increases in staff after automated information systems were installed during the 1970s. Beneath the surface, though, the proportion of clerical, typing and secretarial staff declined by 30 percent.

Industry-wide figures tell the same story, although not necessarily for the same reasons. Between 1975 and 1980, clerical employment fell by 11 percent, while professional–managerial

51

employment increased by over 30 percent. Interestingly, women did not increase their share of positions in this rank. That remained unchanged, at less than 30 percent of professional–managerial employees; yet women are 60 percent of all insurance carrier employees. In addition, the 30 percent increase in professional–managerial employment translated to fewer than four thousand additional jobs, while the 11 percent fall in clerical employment represented a loss of six thousand jobs. In other words, while the occupational profile of this service industry seems to be changing from a pyramid to a pillar shape, the total volume of work is being greatly reduced.

Libraries

The history of computers and computer communications in libraries follows the now familiar pattern: first the automation of individual, essentially recordkeeping functions, such as circulation, ordering and acquisition functions; then the integration of various automated systems as aids to professional library staff, enhancing what they can do and allowing them, at least potentially, to expand library services to become a major growth industry of the information society.

One of the most significant developments in library automation is the American Library of Congress's machine-readable catalogue tapes (MARC), which have become a key element in automated cataloguing systems. Integrated in turn with circulation data systems, they have enabled libraries to increase their services by updating their holdings lists more frequently, among other things. Once in place for library books, the system can be extended into other areas — for example, for staff scheduling and other administrative functions — or to provide service in other locales. At New York University, for example, students can use any computer terminal on campus to query circulation files at the library and find out whether the books they want are available.

Just as the average office-of-the-future worker is more likely to be a professional knowledge worker than an information-handling support worker, librarians of the future promise to become more professional resource and research workers. Some, particularly those with computer skills, could participate in the design of more imaginative and flexible automated index systems to help people find out quickly what knowledge is available. Others might develop computerized library services for special-interest groups or serve as information brokers for corporate customers and ordinary citizens who lack the time or the skill to find their own way through the proliferating array of computerized data bases — close to a thousand in 1982. One such service is already provided by an American library that is on-line with data banks belonging to the *New York Times*, the Lockheed Missile and Space Corporation and the Online Computer Library Centre, which lists more than seven million items. (The Lockheed data bank, which has 1,500 customers, is itself an example of the expanding information industry of providing access to corporate data banks.) In Canada, there are small computer-information firms such as Oracle Information Retrieval Services in Dartmouth, Nova Scotia, run by one person; and there are new services provided by well-established institutions. The University of Toronto Library research desk conducts some 250 searches a month, a figure that is growing steadily. The cost ranges all the way up to $900 and more for an extensive information haul. As well, the National Library in Ottawa has a related project on the drawing board, although it's been stalled there for some time. Called computer retrieval, it would allow the library's Library Documentation Centre to conduct extensive bibliographic reference searches on subjects requested through libraries across the country.

While there are few other Canadian libraries offering this sort of service, a 1981 study by the Economic Council of Canada indicates that there are a wide variety of procedure-related computer applications in evidence. These include recordkeeping (of borrowed books) and cataloguing. It also notes that after a certain amount of preautomation standardization has taken place to accommodate the automation process, libraries were able to expand their workloads fairly rapidly with only a small increase in library staff.

Retail Trade

Retail and wholesale trade have recorded perhaps the most spectacular growth within the overall service-sector boom since the 1950s. Together, they account for nearly a million jobs, with women being largely confined to a few occupations, cashiering most prominent among them.

The food industry, which employs 121,000, was among the pioneer users of computers during the 1950s and 1960s. Computers provided a powerful tool in inventory management, particularly for perishable commodities. The effect on retail food operations was largely hidden until the second wave of automation, although employees had to get used to the new standardized forms, for instance, for recording inventories and price lists. The standard forms were an adaptation to the computer's operating methods; they were also one of the preconditions for supermarket automation. The second precondition, a control function, has been in place since the first cash register.

The final precondition was fulfilled when electronic cash registers began replacing the old-fashioned electromechanical models. Not only did these machines offer 10 to 20 percent faster checkout services, but they provided the necessary medium for computerization. With the incorporation of a microprocessor, the machine was instantly "intelligent." It became the equivalent of a microcomputer terminal, capable of digitizing information, processing it and storing it in electronic form.

The input device in retail trade can be either the cash register keyboard or an optical scanner unit, most often built into the checkout counter. An optical scanner reads the information in the bar code on the item, matches that with price information stored in the store's computer (for automated pricing) and records the item and price both on the cash receipt and in its own memory, as it simultaneously flashes it out on a small display screen.

At the day's end (or at any moment, for that matter), the supermarket's cash registers can be "polled" by either the store's or the supermarket chain's central computer. Amounting to the automatic equivalent of taking a meter reading, this gathering of cash register data will instantly yield vital information for sales-promotion analysis and inventory management as well as day-to-day management and administration. For instance, the data might be analyzed to reveal a store's dollars of business per hour, per cashier and per commodity group. The results can then be compared with the average of other stores as well as with industry standards. Accordingly, employees' hours of work can be changed or reduced, commodity lines altered and management style shifted. To beat competitors and increase sales of electronic cashiering systems, the manufacturers keep enlarging the range of programs (called patterns of action in Charles Babbage's day and simply software today) through which sales data can be processed. One program on the market in the United States even allows the store manager to calculate the most profitable cuts of meat. The implied centralization of decisionmaking is obvious; the meat manager may soon be obsolete.

As the automated store functions are integrated with the company's computer system in an on-line computer communications network, stock can be reordered automatically once cash-register data analysis shows inventories below a certain level. In the United States, the Shaw supermarket chain has reduced storage time by 20 percent in its thirty-eight stores, which are now restocked automatically from its warehouse. In routing more merchandise directly onto the store shelves instead of to the storeroom, the company reports it has also reduced breakage.

As the next step in automation in supermarkets, and in department stores as well, a point-of-sale terminal allows for at least semiautomated payment, either through a store credit card or through the actual transfer of funds electronically. The point-of-sale terminal (POS) can be a separate unit or a modified electronic cash register. The customer's personal identification or debit card, two models of plastic financial authority introduced with automatic teller machines, or a credit card is inserted into the terminal. Once the optical scanner unit has cleared the customer's identity, the terminal's processing unit will relay the billing data to the store's central accounting department for month-end billing, as happens now in department stores, or order the necessary funds moved from the customer's bank account to the store's, or discount the purchasing value left in the renewable electronic cash

55

card and transfer the value to its own account. The latter two payment methods are not yet in commercial use, although discussions between at least one major Canadian bank and a large Canadian supermarket chain on installing such a POS system began in 1980.

With these developments and advances in warehouse automation continuing through the 1980s, the idea of a fully automated self-serve supermarket moves closer to reality. The final step could simply be a security mechanism, so that a product is desensitized as it passes over the optical scanner unit (as already happens in libraries) to neutralize the shoplifting alarm. By then, however, people might be indulging in the self-serve option from home, through videotex teleshopping.

The effects on employment are both direct and indirect. The job of the stock clerk is threatened both by the automation of stocktaking and inventory monitoring and by the efficiencies available through automated reordering; if the goods bypass the stockroom, they also bypass the job functions associated with it.

The effects on cashiers are more subtle. Cashier job hours could be reduced because of the time saved by adding up the bill on electronic cash registers, which are 10 to 20 percent faster than electromechanical ones, and by using the optical scanner unit instead of ringing up each item manually. One study concluded that the following savings could be reaped at peak shopping times: 37 percent increased checker and bagger productivity; 21 percent easier register balancing; 21 percent increased productivity through automatic weighing and pricing; and 14 percent increased performance through reduced errors in price reading and the like.

As well, cashiers are deskilled by the transfer of price information and change calculation into the memory and processing components of the cash register. Like the weaver in the industrial factory, the cashier valued for good price memory and arithmetic efficiency is no longer needed; the cashier becomes a highly replaceable unskilled worker. At McDonald's restaurants, the substitution of product pictures for words on electronic cash registers means that even illiterates are employable.

So many administrative functions are automated or condensed, including cash-flow analysis, overall recordkeeping and almost the entire work of inventory management, that the status of store manager is put in question. Certainly, there is an implied centralization of decisionmaking — from the meat manager to the store manager, and from that person to the regional office or even the supermarket chain head office — as data on the store's sales and stock flows become instantly accessible at a remote head office for processing into information for decisions that the local store manager has traditionally made. The job of store manager could be reduced to the equivalent of a clerical worker, although perhaps with some public-relations window-dressing to compensate for the erosion of real decisionmaking, skill and knowledge.

Fears of widespread job losses recede somewhat before reports that by 1982, no more than 300 out of 31,000 food stores in Canada have installed scanner checkout units, and that no more than 11 percent of department stores had optical scanning or "wanding" by 1979. Still, it has been estimated that up to 90 percent of labour savings associated with automation actually derive from the standardization, streamlining and general reorganization of work that precedes the automation phase itself.

A considerable competitive advantage is won by the first store that becomes automated. In the one American supermarket chain (Giants, in Washington, D.C.) that had completely automated its checkout counters by 1980, productivity gains attributed to the innovations put that chain ahead of the traditional market leader in sales. The automated stores were able to draw peak-hour business away from unautomated competitors on the basis of their faster checkout speeds (37 percent, according to one study).

Certainly, employment in retail trade has begun to level off. As well, overtime has been reduced dramatically and the rise in part-time employment suggests that jobs are being reduced by half. One more mainstay of job growth in the 1960s and 1970s is fading.

Retail trade illustrates two effects of automation additional to the impact on job totals: the loss of privacy and the relentless productivity pressure to which people working at computer equipment can be exposed. In at least one Canadian supermarket chain, daily computer printouts on cashiers' productivity, measured as keystrokes per hour, are posted for all employees to see. Furthermore, those who don't meet the productivity standard are often given shorter work hours. There are cases where some part-time cashiers are working fewer than eight hours a week. Because only about half of them are unionized and the same proportion have only part-time jobs, cashiers are in a poor position to resist these developments.

Telephone Companies

Nowhere is the trend in service industries toward self-service more evident than in telephone companies. This is happening both within the companies, through automation of administrative functions, and as telephone services themselves are delivered on a self-serve basis. In both developments, many thousands of jobs are at stake.

As the cord switchboards have given way to electronic switchboards, more and more operator job functions have been automated. First the function of actually switching calls from one exchange to another was automated. The manual work of plugging and unplugging cords from an electromagnetic switchboard was replaced by automated electronic switching and transmissions, with the operator intervening only briefly for billing information. Since the Traffic Operator Position System (TOPS) was introduced to major Canadian cities between 1979 and 1981, long-distance phoning has become almost completely a self-service activity. Operators only handle the exceptional instances — collect or credit-card calls or other cases requiring special assistance. Even with these calls their involvement is a small part of what it used to be, averaging less than thirty seconds. The caller's number and the call time, which used to be recorded separately on a call ticket and forwarded to the billing department, are now automatically recorded and routed to the accounts department for automatic printout on monthly statements.

Over the course of these developments during the 1970s, the number of telephone operators in the Vancouver area dropped from 1,300 to fewer than 700. In Toronto, operator staff requirements have reportedly been cut by 40 percent. Further job losses result from the centralization of service made possible by automation. In the spring of 1981, Bell Canada closed four regional offices across Quebec, displacing 100 telephone operators in such a centralization move. Telephone operator employment dropped by 32 percent in Britain and by 25 percent in Austria when automated long-distance calling was introduced to those countries.

More jobs are threatened with the automation of both directory assistance and operator intercept, anticipated during the 1980s. Operators who normally intercept calls to disconnected or otherwise nonworking numbers are being replaced by computer-assembled messages explaining the problem and providing helpful information. The computer-assembled voice works on the same principle as boilerplate storage in word processing: stock pieces of stored messages are pieced together according to the standardized prescription for the given situation.

Still more jobs are threatened when the automated call-handling functions are integrated with other automated information-handling systems in an overall communications or teleprocessing network. In an example of one teleprocessing system in an American phone company, service orders, connection, disconnection, billing and bill adjustment, relocation and even trouble-shooting have been integrated into one on-line system, allowing the customer-service representative to perform any task within any of these service areas on the video display terminal at his or her desk, saving time, paper and innumerable clerical steps. One company, Winter Park Telephone of Florida, has reportedly cut its service representative staff in half since implementing this system.

For telephone operators, a classic female job ghetto with women holding 90 percent of the jobs, the future is not encouraging. Not only is there less and less work, but people are being squeezed into an ever smaller and less skilled job description and thus being further cut off from the chance to move forward to other work. Besides being deskilled, operators are being downgraded as people. Computer monitoring of their job performance both invades their privacy and exaggerates the importance of quantity over quality in one's work. For instance, the computer records the number of transactions executed per customer and the number of customers served, but not whether satisfactory service was given. As well, operators are subtly diverted from responding to customers to responding to the computer system. Instead of plugging in to incoming calls from customers wanting assistance, operators

59

now passively receive their work through the computerized call-handling control centre. As soon as operators finish one call, another is automatically beamed to their headsets.

Other Industries

Name an industry in the service sector and, as long as there is a lot of information work involved, one can almost predict where productivity can be improved, jobs eliminated and occupations transformed through automation. In hotels, reservations, room charges and other service charges are all handled, processed and recorded automatically. Cashiers can be bypassed as waiters and waitresses operate cash registers which are not only simplified through electronics but are also able to transmit charges to front-office information systems and to perform the same range of data processing administrative functions as in a supermarket. A British paper on computers in hotel management concluded that payroll savings of up to 20 percent could result. Most of the savings would be expressed as reduced clerical workers, the paper said; however, integrated automated information systems in hotels would presumably threaten traditional administrative and other middle-management jobs as well.

In hospitals, initial computer applications during the 1960s and early 1970s were for large data processing requirements associated with payroll and central patient records. Microprocessors installed since have allowed for smaller information-handling functions to be automated, such as recording of drug and pharmacy orders and patient histories. These have subsequently been integrated into larger on-line computer communications systems in large hospitals, allowing hospital personnel to consult and update central data files on terminals located throughout the hospital. By 1978, according to a study of computer innovations in Canadian service industries conducted by the Economic Council of Canada, a third of Canadian hospitals were using data processing systems for administrative or clinical functions.

There is also the snowball factor. Once an on-line, integrated computer communications system is in place, new automated information systems and services can be plugged into it, multiplying cost savings and potential job losses. Consider the impact on jobs in drugstores once pharmacists adopt the information-service package developed by a drug wholesaler in the American midwest. When a pharmacist has keyed the customer's prescription into the computer terminal, the central computer will process it (at a rate of twelve transactions per minute) through these steps: first it will check the drug against the patient's profile of prior and outstanding prescriptions to look for negative drug interactions, to ensure, for a refill request, that refills are allowed, and to update the customer's file. Then the prescription is automatically priced and billing instructions on file followed (credit card, medicare, third-party or other billing), with the relevant data sent to the funding sources and duly recorded as well. Finally, label information, including price and dosage instructions, is printed automatically, and in the language requested by the customer, onto the label emitted by the terminal at the drugstore using the system.

It seems that the three major trends in employment effects of computerization in the service sector are extensions of the pattern identified in the previous chapter: first, the galloping growth of jobs traditionally held by women has been checked and even reversed as the delivery of services and support work generally is automated. Yet women continue to orient themselves to this type of work and be confined within it. Furthermore, the number of women in the work force is expected to increase by some 2 million over the next decade, but without the traditional mainstays of female employment there to receive them.

Second, traditional middle-level administration and management work is being automated, and being replaced by work of a much more technical and professional nature. And at professional and senior-management levels, work is being intensified, as computer aids boost the scope and standards of performance, and a knowledge of computers, if not actual computer skills, is required. Employers might have trouble filling their increasingly high-skill human-resource needs in the years ahead given that most growth in the labour force in the 1980s and 1990s will be not from young professional graduates from universities but from people already into their working lives, particularly women, who are being displaced by the automation phase of the technology.

Women might have difficulty qualifying for these new jobs because of the widening skills gap between the two groups of occupations — support and professional–managerial. This, the third major trend, suggests an ironic coincidence of two employment problems occurring simultaneously: a severe skills shortage in Canadian industry and severe structural unemployment as a mismatch develops between the skills of the labour force and the rising skill demands of industry. Women stand to suffer the most from this skills shortfall. Not only do they lack many of the skills and professional orientation, but with the automation of traditional middle-management work, they've lost a possible bridge or stepping stone out of the clerical support jobs where they've historically been concentrated and for which they've been groomed and educated. In identifying this skills gap as the major issue threatening the transition from the mechanical to the computer age, the study *Women and the Chip* concluded that unless special measures (training and occupational bridging) were immediately implemented, as many as a million Canadian women could be unemployed by 1990.

At the same time, as many if not more men could be unemployed, as a result of factory automation.

Still, there's a lot to be said for working with robots. They're never in a bad mood, they don't bore you with their problems and they never ask to borrow a few bucks till payday.

4

Automation
and Blue-Collar Jobs

P ackaged in microchip form, the
second wave of automation is deluging Canadian industry. In
sawmills, microprocessor control systems guide saws and marshal
cut boards to the planing equipment. In garment factories, similar
systems automatically stitch seams and sew on buttons. At the
International Harvester machinery plant in Hamilton, Ontario,
single robots are doing work that previously employed six steelworkers. And in the industry that produces microchips —
microelectronics — the Brockville, Ontario, firm Computer Assembly Systems Ltd. runs a completely automated process for
assembling components of printed circuit boards.

These are just a few examples of how automation is taking over
blue-collar jobs, and it seems inevitable that more automation in
industry is on its way. Moreover, Canada is lagging behind its
competitors in the international race to exploit the new technology;
and if we don't stay abreast of developments, jobs may disappear

anyway as unautomated companies that become uncompetitive reduce their operations or simply go under. It's this international aspect that makes automation a more complex problem in industry than in white-collar work, which tends to be more domestic in its orientation. Since manufacturing in Canada employs 20 percent of the work force, with most of the 2.5 million jobs concentrated in central Canada, where economic growth is expected to be minimal for at least a decade, industry's transition from the mechanical age into the computer age deserves watchful concern.

Illustrating the scope of the problem, a major article in *Business Week* magazine in the summer of 1981 estimated that 45 million jobs in North America would be either lost, deskilled or otherwise transformed through automation in industry over the next 10 to 15 years. The prestigious Rand Corporation in the United States predicts that by the year 2000 only 2 percent of the North American labour force will be employed in manufacturing industries.

The *Business Week* article reported that American industry plans to triple its spending on automation by 1985. General Motors is on record as planning to have 90 percent of its car-making equipment run by computer control by 1990. General Electric plans to have 1,000 robots in its household appliance plants by 1990. American textile firms are engaged in a major modernization drive with the objective of eliminating some 300,000 relatively low-paid production jobs through automation.

Japanese achievements dwarf those planned in the United States. In 1981, Japan produced some 20,000 robots, in factories that are themselves largely run by robots. Toshiba Tungalloy's new plant operates full tilt through the night without a single worker on site. A similarly modern robot plant operated by Fujitsu Fanuc produces 100 robots a month with a fifth of the workers it previously required. The Japanese Robot Manufacturing Association forecasts that robot production will increase at 24 percent a year through the 1980s.

Broadening the picture from robots to microelectronics in general, there's the Mitsubishi corporation, which in 1981 was reportedly producing seven times its 1970 output with a work force only 15 percent larger, and the giant Toshiba, which has plans to reduce its labour force from 2,500 to 500 by 1984. Matsushita

Electric reported a 2,900 percent improvement in productivity in its vacuum cleaner plant when it replaced 200 workers by a computer, a robot team and four human monitors.

As American industry rushes to catch up to Japan, Canadian industry is scrambling to even enter the race. Relative strength in robotics provides at least a partial indication of these countries' positions in the computerization competition in industry. In 1980, while there were no more than two or three hundred robots in Canada, there were estimated to be three thousand in the United States. But in Japan, the world leader in robot manufacturing and chief supplier to North American industry, an International Metalworkers Federation report estimated that there were 75,000 robots in use. The comparison is somewhat flawed, however, since the Japanese definition of robot is considered more liberal than the North American criteria. Even by the stricter definition, the estimated 14,000 robots in Japan still represent more than four times the number throughout the much larger American industrial system.

Canada's Disadvantage in Automation

These developments, and their implied consequences for factory workers, are unfolding within the discouraging framework of Canada's chronically weak and backward manufacturing sector. This itself is largely due to and is further compounded by the high foreign ownership of that sector. Not only is 60 percent of the total manufacturing sector foreign-owned or -controlled, but control over some of the linchpin industries of the computer age lies beyond Canadian borders.

In the crucial category of electronics, seventy-two of the top 100 Canadian firms are foreign-controlled as well. Electronics is the foundation of all computer and communications innovations associated with the office and factory of the future; yet even the largest Canadian firm, Northern Telecom, is considered only medium-sized by world standards. This weakness in Canadian manufacturing translates into dependency on others, as the trade figures on supplying the office of the future bear out. In 1981, Canada's trade deficit in office equipment stood at $1.2 billion, and the Minister of Industry, Trade and Commerce predicted it would reach $5 billion by 1982. Dollars that could have built Canadian industry are drained out of the economy.

So while it's been estimated that by the late 1980s, electronics will be the world's fourth largest industry — behind automobiles, steel and chemicals — Canada's stake in it remains small, accounting for only 2.3 percent of world production, and for less than 2 percent of Canada's gross national product. The picture could improve, however, as governments pour millions of dollars in aid, including a $12 million federal program for office-of-the-future manufacturing, into the electronics sector.

Pressure to use technology to improve the productivity of Canadian industry has been strong since a 1978 Science Council of Canada report (titled *The Weakest Link*) documented the precarious position in which the sector's low productivity left the entire Canadian economy, to say nothing of the 2.5 million Canadians employed in manufacturing. Subsequently, a 1980 survey of Canadian manufacturing companies, commissioned by the federal Department of Industry, Trade and Commerce, found 90 percent of them convinced that computer-controlled manufacturing systems were an urgent modernization priority if they were to remain competitive. In 1980, manufacturing accounted for most of the computer installations in Canada, although by then the service industries were ahead of manufacturing in the rate of installations.

In another telling development, the federal government in 1981 set up the Canadian Industrial Renewal Board with some $270 million to help modernize the clothing, textile and footwear industries, which currently employ more than 200,000 Canadians, concentrated in the urban centres of Quebec and Ontario and, to a lesser extent, in Winnipeg. Many of these centres are in a prolonged economic slump and aren't expected to grow significantly through the 1980s. Yet in the clothing industry, which employs 55,000 in Quebec alone, the use of import tariff barriers to protect these jobs against cheaper imports has been estimated to cost Canadians $500 million a year in higher prices.

Yet another debilitating result of foreign ownership in Canada's manufacturing sector is that the proportion of research and development funding that flows from government sources is higher in Canada than in almost any other industrialized country, but total R&D funding is less than 1 percent of gross national product, well below the percentage of most other industrialized countries. This is because industry's R&D funding in Canada is almost negligible. Very simply, foreign-owned companies do their R&D at home and export the technology to their Canadian branch plants. Not only do these plants pay for this technology (in fees paid to head office for engineering and other professional services), but they are trapped permanently behind the lines of technological innovation. Although government funds are being diverted toward R&D in the electronics area, the totals are almost insignificant compared to the sums devoted annually to high-technology development in competitor countries. As a minimum, R&D should be targetted to represent 2.5 percent of GNP by 1990, with industry carrying at least half of that investment responsibility, and with ownership of any new technology developed staying within Canada as well.

Once the decision to modernize has been made, the automation process can proceed fairly rapidly. The preconditions are already in place: most factory work has long ago been organized into standard procedures, with control over those procedures located in machines and assembly lines; a high degree of mechanization makes automation simply another step in a technological continuum rather than a major undertaking, as is often the case in office automation. Third, the electrical power system merely needs to be modified so that computers and chips can take control over the mechanical processes.

There are three stages in the development of the fully automated "factory of the future": in the first phase, individual functions are automated. These will include parts assembly and materials handling on the factory floor; stock monitoring and movement in the warehouse; drafting work and other aspects of product design work in the engineering departments; product inspection and testing both on and off the production line; packaging, labelling and storing in the back of the factory; and production scheduling, budget management and all the other functions associated with automated information systems in the front office.

In the second phase, these automated functions are integrated into modules or subsystems classified, depending on their composition, as either flexible manufacturing workstations (for instance, for subassembly and machine tooling) or computer aids (for instance, computer-aided design or inventory management). The phrase "computer-aided" signals the possible start of the third innovation phase, when integrated systems are applied toward new activities, perhaps to generate new economic activity and new sources of employment. This innovation phase, however, depends more on an enabling investment decision than on the enabling technology itself. It will also depend on employment developments through the first two phases. If the pattern that emerged in the office and the service sector — a skills gap between the people being displaced by automation and the new jobs being created by computer aids — continues in the manufacturing sector, the potential for computer-aided manufacturing to produce new and enriched work might be blocked for lack of skilled Canadians.

Resource Industries

Developments in the primary sector illustrate the difference in scope between the first and second waves of automation. In resource industries, where first wave computer systems automated large-scale processes such as smelting, refining, pulp processing and papermaking, the microprocessors of the second wave are now being applied to automate control and feedback functions such as temperature monitoring to lend "intelligence" to those continuous-flow automated processes. They're also extending the scope of automation, to assembly-like activities.

On farms, microprocessors added to electromechanical livestock feeding systems automatically cut off the flow of chopped silage and grain into feed troughs. In innovative grain-harvesting combines, microprocessor controls in the threshing unit monitor the speed of operation to ensure that grain is not lost out the back of the machine. In mines, automation is extended to loading ore into mine carts and controlling conveyor systems, and in fish- and meat-packing plants, conveyor systems and packaging are automated.

In a MacMillan Bloedel sawmill in Port Alberni, British Columbia, a microprocessor-equipped camera measures each incoming log, matches this information with 15,000 possible cutting patterns stored in the mill's computer memory, slots the saw plan most appropriate to the log's dimensions into the saw's microchip processing unit and, presto, the log is cut according to that plan. Since installing this system (at a mere $51 million), the company has been getting roughly 10 percent more yield per log and has reduced its mill work force by forty people. In another British Columbia sawmill, some twelve jobs per shift were eliminated after the introduction of an automatic bin sorter that identifies and sorts lumber by grade, length and width.

Twenty-two thousand workers in British Columbia, 11,000 Quebecers and thousands more in other provinces depend on the forest industry for their employment. In many cases, they live in single industry towns, making them even more vulnerable to the job-cutting effects of automation.

Manufacturing

With most of Canadian manufacturing restricted to short production runs for the relatively small domestic market, very little first wave automation could be cost-justified. As well, most applications were confined to the manufacture of basic parts, in processes such as moulding, while Canadian manufacturing activity has historically concentrated on assembling parts that have been manufactured by parent companies or other American companies who have the economies of scale necessary to support a major computer installation.

Second wave automation based on the microchip takes a number of often unique forms in manufacturing, each producing its own effects on jobs. Two of these affect the manufacture of parts: the replacement of electromechanical parts with electronic parts, and numeric control. Numerically controlled machines automate the moulding of parts, and numerically controlled tools automate the machining of metal into parts such as bolts.

Numeric control uses the same principle as Jacquard's loom in the nineteenth century. A sequence, such as a series of positions and angles, is represented by holes punched in a tape which, on being automatically read, tells the computer how to position the cutting tool. Numeric control is less flexible than a computer-controlled system because any new programming requires that a new tape be punched.

An international report on the labour effects of chip technology concludes that numerically controlled machine tools can replace two or more conventional tools, reduce tooling and fixture costs by up to 70 percent and reduce unit labour requirements by between 25 and 80 percent, depending on the degree of integration.

In the United States, where numerically controlled machine tools account for a third of parts manufacturing, this technology is partly blamed for the roughly 15 percent a year attrition rate among metalworkers and machinists since the late 1970s. The remaining work is a dramatic comedown for tool and die makers, the elite craftsmen of manufacturing. The punched tape removes the knowledge and artisan skill associated with reading blueprints and translating their specifications into machine-tool calibrations. A person with such qualifications is now either bypassed or deskilled to the level of machinist.

Besides taking its toll in job totals and job challenge, the technological change erodes morale. A former craftsman now running numerically controlled machines was quoted in a report as saying he felt frustrated because all the skill, knowledge and intuition he had used in controlling the machine was still in his head, but now untapped.

The machinists' work is being automated as well, because numeric control takes over the task of running the machine tools. There is still work for maintenance machinists, although even for them, retraining and adjustment is required to change from essentially mechanical skills to electrical ones. Finally, numeric control automates the work of machine-tool operators who normally set up, recalibrate and adjust the machines used in metal forming, drilling, threading and turning the metal parts. Now this is all done automatically through the computer or numeric paper tapes, with the operator merely monitoring the process and requiring only a little on-the-job training to know when to call in the maintenance machinist to correct whatever goes wrong.

A University of Michigan study of skill shifts associated with numeric control found that training time had been reduced by a factor of twelve: four months to train a machinist instead of four years. Not surprisingly, there is evidence that earnings in these occupations are slipping from the premium status they have traditionally held.

It isn't expected that Canada will see massive installations of numeric control systems, because of the concentration of Canadian industry on parts assembly.

The clothing industry provides a related illustration of second wave automation in the manufacturing process itself (as distinct from the assembly process, for instance). In that industry, automated contour seamers, profile-stitching machines and automated button-sewing systems complete with automatic button feeding have increased productivity and reduced jobs and skill needs as well. The contour seamer and profile stitching systems feature a photoelectric sensor and stored program sequences to guide the material automatically through the sewing mechanism. The craft of guiding the material properly has been absorbed into the computer program, which is stored in locally controlled memory (programmable read-only memory) units. According to a United States Labor Bureau study of automation in the clothing industry, these systems can reduce the labour content of making shirt collars by up to 64 percent. They also reduce the training requirements for machine operators, allowing manufacturers to draw on "a larger labour pool," the report says.

The second example of automation in manufacturing also touches on assembly work. When electronic components replace electromechanical parts, human work is reduced in two ways: first, by the automation of manufacturing the parts themselves — through the same planar etching process used to manufacture the first integrated circuit; and secondly, by automating what had been a manual process of assembling the sequences of mechanical parts into subassembly components. Essentially the subassembly aspect of manufacturing work is absorbed into the initial manufacturing of parts, thereby truncating the manufacturing process and truncating employment opportunities as well.

Perhaps the most dramatic illustration of this effect occurred in the watch industry when digital watches from Japan and Hong

73

Kong usurped the leadership position in the world watch market that Switzerland had traditionally enjoyed. With digital watches, sequences of up to 1,000 intricate mechanical parts have been replaced by a handful of simple microelectronic components that are themselves produced automatically. Because of the digital watch's vastly lower production costs, 46,000 jobs disappeared from the Swiss watch industry within two years as the new models took the consumer world by storm. Not that the 46,000 jobs reappeared in the Far East; only a fraction of that number were created, because the time-consuming and taxing work of assembling the sequences of mechanical parts had been replaced by the automated reproduction of those sequences in an integrated circuit.

An additional labour elimination due to this type of substitution is in repair work and maintenance. When an electronic watch part breaks, you simply pop in a new one.

Results similar to the blow to the Swiss watch industry have been produced in the manufacturing of telephone and telecommunications equipment, sewing machines and cash registers. National Cash Register reduced its European work force from 37,000 in 1970 to 18,000 in 1975 as it switched its manufacturing from electromechanical cash registers to the electronic models that are revolutionizing the retail trade. In its 1975 annual report to shareholders, the company noted that the new cash register had only a quarter of the labour content of its predecessor. A European survey of manufacturing employment with microelectronics had an only slightly less drastic conclusion: microelectronics-based equipment needs about half the manufacturing work force required for producing electromechanical equipment. The Swedish company Ericsson, which produces telephone exchanges, reduced employment from 15,000 to 10,000 over three years in the late 1970s when it switched over from electromechanical to electronic models. When it terminates the last lines of electromechanical equipment, it expects the work force to be half what it was before the changeover. Western Electric in the United States has reduced its manufacturing work force by some 50 percent in a similar switchover.

This development also effectively shifts the focal point of employment away from the parts-assembly stage, which has traditionally been the most labour-intensive, to the component manufacturing stage ana, within that, to the manufacturer of silicon chips and integrated circuits. Again, the implications for Canada are a further weakening of a manufacturing sector that, weak in parts manufacture and particularly in production of electronics components such as chips and integrated circuits, must rely on imports of these products.

There is considerable erosion of skill in this type of automation as well. When Singer replaced 350 mechanical parts with one microelectronic component in switching to an electronic sewing machine, it no longer needed a skilled craftsperson able to assemble those 350 tiny parts. That skill and experience was absorbed into the computer program that generated the microprocessor automatically.

Robots

Moving from component manufacturing to the assembly stage, robots are perhaps the most dramatic innovation that people associate with factory automation, and with good reason. Designed and constructed to do the work that humans do, they are seen as human-like; they are, however, no more like humans than the workers they replace are like robots, although many workers may feel they *have* become robots from doing repetitive, essentially drudgery-type work. The point is worth pondering, especially since the word robot is derived from the Czech word for drudgery work. One has to wonder why work can't be organized so drudgery jobs don't exist in the first place.

The simplest robot falls somewhat short of the cuddly humanoids featured in science fiction films. But real robots don't need locomotion or flashing lights. They are designed simply to do routine manipulative tasks such as painting and welding. They look like pieces of machinery, often consisting of movable arms and claw-like "hands" with welding torches or spray-paint nozzles clenched in their grip.

The simplest robots are reasonably affordable — less than $25,000 each — and getting cheaper all the time, as microelectronic components continue to plummet in price while, as a robot salesperson might point out, labour costs continue to climb.

Indeed, there are many reports of robots that have better productivity than humans, or, to look at it from a labour point of view, that can replace three workers here, five there. An article in the engineering magazine *Spectrum* pointed out that 1980 automotive labour costs averaged fourteen dollars an hour, whereas a certain model of robot, amortized over eight years, averaged only four dollars an hour. Further, the article noted, by 1990 the robot's costs could drop to the equivalent of one dollar an hour, compared to labour costs that could rise as high as thirty dollars an hour. Even if predictions like these turn out to be wrong, they'll likely influence factory owners anxious to increase productivity and cut costs, especially when the robot salesperson goes on to list other benefits. For instance, a robot can be retrained simply by pushing the "teach" button and guiding the robot arm through a new series of motions. These motions are recorded in the robot's memory to be repeated, without mistakes, whenever it's called upon to do so.

The next step up from the simple robots are "servo" robots. Servo is short for servomechanism, a device in which the action is achieved by a continual comparison between the existing position and the desired position. The difference, if any, is used to drive the device toward that desired position. In a model airplane, the servo mechanism translates the frantic jerkings of the joystick in the control box clutched by the operator into smooth mechanical motions, such as lowering the flaps. On a grander scale, automated servomechanisms operated the joints of the Canadarm on the American space shuttle Columbia. Servo robots, more complex and capable of a more dexterous type of assembly, can be programmed to do more detailed processes and "remember" each sequence by storing it in their memories. They can also be reprogrammed, so that a servo welder can work on a Ford Pinto one minute and a Mustang the next.

The auto industry is a leader in robotics use in North America. The commonest uses are spot welding, machine loading, die casting, spray painting and, increasingly, assembly. General Motors plan to install 14,000 robots in its North American plants by 1990 breaks out like this: 1,500 for painting, 2,700 for welding, 5,000 for parts assembly, 4,000 for loading machine tools and 800 for parts transfer.

By that time, of course, robots may have become even more advanced. Already there are robots with "sight" and "feel" sensor devices, incorporating microprocessors, that can pick up parts and actually align them within a tolerance no wider than the thickness of a human hair. But there are still bugs to be worked out in these sophisticated models that might keep them beyond the reach of commercial application for some time.

Simple microprocessor-equipped sensing devices are the key factor opening the way to the integration phase of factory automation. Here, similar processes that have been separately automated or made "intelligent" through computerization are integrated, with sensor advices often acting as the glue or coordinating agent between the functions. On the factory floor, this stage allows truly "intelligent" robots to be placed in integrated workstations. Such robots respond to and act according to the information they receive through their sensing devices, not a pre-set program. The PUMA (programmable universal manipulator for assembly) robot is an example of such a subassembly integrated workstation. It is used in some American General Motors plants to assemble electronic components such as dashboard light fixtures. With microprocessor-equipped sensing devices and servo manipulating devices, the robot unit can unload one subassembly component from its assembly mechanism with one gripper unit while another stands by ready to load the next batch of assembly parts.

With few robots yet installed in North American industry, information on employment effects is scanty and, without a pattern to judge by, potentially misleading. According to an International Metalworkers Federation report, however, 211 jobs were lost in American General Motors plants after eighty-five paint-spraying robots were installed in the late 1970s. The same report estimated that each robot displaces an average of five workers. In one Swedish car plant, robots reportedly paid for themselves in eighteen months.

Still greater productivity gains become possible with increasing integration. After the intelligent robot workstations, the next step up is to the integrated subsystem, sometimes called a flexible manufacturing system. The difference between the two degrees of integration is similar to that between a word processing workstation and a fully integrated management information system with company-wide data files, electronic mail and messaging.

The Japanese are world leaders in this more mature stage of integration; in fact, most of North American industry appears still to be at the automation stage or the first level of integration, the workstation only. In Japan, where industry analysis of pioneering integrated systems boasts as much as 75 percent savings in production costs, the Japanese government is playing an active role.

In one project sponsored by the Japanese Ministry of International Trade and Industry (MITI), five automated functions are being incorporated into one flexible manufacturing system. These are fabricating parts in reprogrammable dies, machining these parts, treating and further machining them by laser, robot assembly of the finished parts and finally, automated inspection of the final product. MITI hopes that by 1985, as much as 20 percent of Japan's total factory output will be produced in flexible manufacturing systems.

Automation Subsystems

Off the factory floor, other functions are being automated and integrated into subsystems as well. Each of these can be identified as components of the fully integrated factory of the future. These subsystems of the automated factory fall into six broad categories:

- In corporate management, automated inventory and budget management, customer-order handling, invoicing and other management information systems;
- In product design, including computer-aided design drawing and testing for durability, stress and so on;
- In manufacturing process planning, computer-aided materials handling and scheduling of manufacture;
- In the manufacturing process itself, where numerically controlled and computer-controlled machine tools are joining automated lathes, milling, boring machines, pattern and fabric cutting, welding, brazing, plating, spray painting and assembly;
- In the quality-control phase, automated testing of electronic

components and sensor units for pattern recognition and grading;

- In the final phase of packaging and delivery, computer-controlled packaging, bottling, labelling and weighing, plus automated order picking, automated label reading, routing and other aspects of automated warehousing.

A brief look at several elements in these subsystems will show how automation is reaching into every corner of employment in manufacturing industries.

Computer-aided design is a combination of automated data processing (for calculation and analysis), information handling and graphics. At its most elementary level, computer-aided design automates the drafting of design blueprints, the equivalent of automated printing in a word processor. This capability, which effectively puts draftspersons out of work, is thought to be quite widely employed in North American industry. At the next stage of sophistication, with data processing capabilities added, the design engineer will be able to test different materials and costing variables to produce the most cost-effective design. At the most sophisticated level, hypothesizing and testing models, with variables taking a wide range of values, are incorporated into computer programs. The result is similar to the budget models used in office automation. Just as these administrative tools can displace office administrators and management accountants from the automated office, so these computer aids might displace design engineers and technicians as well as draftspersons from the automated factory.

The automated warehouse subsystem is almost a textbook illustration of the process of technological change and of how it affects work. When warehouses were first built, the man running one was king of that small domain; only he knew where everything was. He also needed considerable organizational skills and was rightly proud of how efficiently he stored items in their logical places. More modern warehouses, with pallets and forklifts, transferred some of that storage expertise into the design of the building and parts. Standardized forms for recording both the location of boxes in the warehouses and their contents eroded that expertise still further. Soon anybody could run a warehouse, and now they run themselves. A 560,000-square-foot warehouse in the United

States, which services seventy-five supermarkets, is entirely automated and managed by a computer.

A Japanese firm, Murata Machinery, is marketing an automated materials-handling system that includes two driverless carts, pallet changers and software. The carts move through the factory guided by wires implanted in the floor. It results in "huge labour savings," according to an industry magazine report. How huge is huge? An automated brewery warehouse in Japan employs three people and is twice the size of its predecessor, which employed thirty.

In another example of automated functions integrated into a subsystem for greater productivity, a nonprofit applied-research institute called Computer Aided Manufacturing International (of which McGill University and the University of New Brunswick are members) is perfecting a computer-aided process planning and factory-management system that promises to reduce production time by 50 percent and total production costs by 30 percent.

When all the subsystems are in place, they can be plugged together to form flexible manufacturing systems, the next stage of integration. Here, automated functions are arranged in a hierarchy of computer control ranging from the large mainframe computer down through a series of minicomputers (sometimes called satellites) at the subsystem level and microprocessors in servo units and sensory devices. Flexibility and autonomy (for batch assembly and parts alignment, for example) at the local level are possible, while economies of scale and overall coordination are achieved through the larger mainframe computer and data banks. Flexible manufacturing systems are credited with multiple sources of labour savings and efficiencies, and are expected to become widespread during the late 1980s and 1990s.

In Japan, a manufacturer of machine tools, Yamazaki, has invested $15 million toward integrating materials handling and back-up information handling with a cluster of eighteen machine tools, such as numerically controlled lathes and metal forms. The tools are housed in a rotating workstation structured as a rotating drum and supported within a hierarchy of on-line computer control. A host mainframe computer maintains overall control over scheduling and operations while satellite computers regulate the transportation of parts and semiassembled products from machine to machine, and other computers handle such automated office functions as financial reporting, inventory management and production control.

A Montreal-based, foreign-owned company specializing in cosmetics manufacturing and marketing spent ten years in the pre-automation work of standardizing its operations and the related structures and forms. Initial computerization in the actual production process (automated process control) and of accounting and other statistical functions was followed by microprocessor-based extensions of automation. These included automatic conveying of products for packaging, automatic labelling and semi-automatic warehouse operations. By 1981, the company had integrated all the information handling work, from processing incoming orders to labelling the products and issuing invoices and transportation waybills. As soon as the standardized order form is read by the optical scanner in the mail room, the information in digitized form speeds simultaneously in a number of directions: to the manufacturing process planning people, who ensure there is sufficient inventory on hand and adjust personnel schedules where necessary; to the warehouse, where inventory levels are automatically adjusted as the production materials are ferried manually into position in the processing plant. The information also goes to the production control centre, where the production run will be programmed and scheduled, and to the billing department, where an invoice and shipping order are automatically generated.

The information-work nature of this example is representative of the number of jobs in Canadian manufacturing that are associated with marketing, distributing and managing, rather than manufacturing as such. It is in this type of work that automation will likely reduce jobs in the years ahead.

There is another, rather unique issue arising from automation of information work in manufacturing firms, particularly foreign-owned firms. Called "transborder data flows," the issue is an extension of the vulnerability Canadian industry has chronically suffered as a result of foreign ownership and control in the Canadian economy. It involves the transmission of electronic data (on sales, market tests or, in the resource sector, exploration tests) south of the border to parent company head offices, rather than to branch offices in Canada, for processing into information on the basis of which important decisions will be made. The pattern arises naturally from the capacities of integrated information systems; yet it threatens Canadians' jobs as well as their decisionmaking autonomy.

For Canada at least, the fully integrated factory of the future is thought to be far down the road. Linking the various subsystems is considered to be the key problem and a formidable one at that. It is possible, too, that the problem of foreign ownership will complicate this process, as parent companies may wish to concentrate their automation efforts at home, leaving their Canadian branch plants to shift for themselves, possibly becoming too uncompetitive to survive.

Employment Erosion

As in the service-sector industries, the final or net employment outcome will hinge largely on the third, innovation phase in applying computer technology to industry. Even when this phase begins, it won't necessarily provide much new employment. For instance, through advances in computer-aided design, one avenue of new activity might be virtual self-serve manufacturing. On entering the car dealership, customers would sit before a VDT and mix and match parts from a variety of choices in the electronic catalogue to virtually custom design their own cars. In this scenario, customers would only require the relatively unskilled assistance of a salesperson, directing them how to use the computer terminals. Yet an alternative implementation scenario, perhaps one designed with the involvement of the persons actually being affected by the technology, could yield more, and enriched, employment opportunities. Here, an engineer would use computer-aided design as a tool in creating truly unique and individualized car models.

This demonstrates once again how much the innovation phase depends on the enabling decisions, who is making them and according to what values and priorities; the technology is only one part of the equation.

Without the frontier of the third phase, the development of new industries by applying integrated computer communications systems toward enhancing human creativity, the professional and technical people who are in such high demand while the automated systems are being installed could automate themselves out of work once those systems are in place. This is thought to have happened in Boeing, a major aeronautics firm that is among the world leaders in automated manufacturing and is credited with having an integrated computer-aided design and computer-aided manufacturing (CAD-CAM) system itself. In 1979 and 1980, it laid off thousands of engineering, professional and technical staff associated with design and development work and staff from middle management. The layoffs coincided with a continuing upsurge in research and design contracts, which the company was attracting in part because of the competitive advantage its computer-aided design systems conferred on it.

On the other hand, a company that developed an automated information system for real-time inventory update and financial controls is now selling this system as a software service product that can be run on the minicomputers of client companies. There is a suggestion of new job growth in this information product, although the implied ripple effect might destroy middle-management jobs associated with that administration work in the client company.

The innovation phase will also depend on employment developments during the first two phases. If workers whose jobs and skills are being taken over by automation are able to learn how to work with the automated systems and are given the chance to do so, they could themselves become an enabling force for the innovation phase. Putting that potential into effect, in the form of innovative new activity, would of course depend on a dramatic increase in worker rights — such as the right to participate in the design of new jobs for continuous employment. Such rights are nonexistent under Canadian labour legislation and are only beginning to surface in contract negotiations.

The pattern already identified in the white-collar world suggests, however, that many blue-collar workers could simply be left behind, with skills made redundant by automation, and their

83

labour made surplus to the demand for a relatively few individuals needed to resolve industry's skill-shortage problem.

Unfortunately, there has been very little research on changes in employment and occupational shifts in factories as the result of automation. However, from the isolated case reports and trends in job totals, it seems that the effects are much the same in both manufacturing and service industries. Just as people who handle, manipulate and process information are likely to be most negatively affected by white-collar automation, so the blue-collar workers who handle, manipulate and process materials are likely to suffer the most from factory automation. In a study of eight companies in the United States, Germany and Italy involved in machinery production, there was an overall 20 percent decline in employment between 1969 and 1978. The percentage of production workers within these companies dropped from an average of over 40 percent to just over 25 percent. In Canada, a study of computerization in the petroleum industry found that only 30 percent of the employees are now involved in production work; the others are involved in information-related work, running and designing the computerized systems that in turn run the refining operations, for instance.

Besides the erosion of production jobs, there's also a migration of employment away from the shop or factory floor. Just as the locus of control moves from the person to the machine when tool and die makers' and machinists' work is automated through numerically controlled machines, so the locus of employment moves from the shop floor to the office of the design engineers and computer programmers, usually nonunionized.

Just as in the white-collar areas, when automated functions are tied into an integrated network, more work, knowledge and skill, as well as personal initiative and control, can then be taken over. This applies not only to the production workers, but also to the warehouse manager, the quality control supervisor and the draftsperson or even design engineer.

Factory foremen could become redundant, not only because the number of people working in the factory is dropping, but also because computer monitoring of machine cycles eliminates the need for supervision. It also destroys the foreman's traditional discretionary power to go along with staff who push themselves at their machine tools all morning and let the machine "cut air" a bit in a somewhat lazier pace through the afternoon. Now computers monitor the machine-tool power supply and are alerted by reduced power flows if the machines are not working at the usual level. Thus alerted, the computer signals to the foreman that it's time to discipline the worker, foiling the foreman's willingness to be flexible, with obvious implications for plant morale as well as self-management on the factory floor.

The industry skills profile seems to be changing from a squat pyramid with a skills "ladder" to something more skewed, with a mass of deskilled people at the bottom, a few skilled maintenance and repair people in the middle and a few highly skilled professionals at the top.

The labour elimination in industry isn't restricted to the factory itself. In the telephone industry (which, in addition to automating much of its service delivery, has taken advantage of electronics parts substitution in manufacturing), installation work is reduced to insignificance. In fact, it has been so simplified that it's become, like basic banking, a self-serve activity. In telephone stores in most cities and towns, Canadians bypass installers by picking up their own phone sets to plug in at home.

Maintenance and repair work is reduced, and what remains is effectively deskilled because fixing is increasingly being reduced to substituting one microelectronic component for another, as easily as replacing lightbulbs. Diagnostic equipment, which might soon teach new operators with a built-in computer-aided instructional program, achieves the same deskilling effect as the mail-sorting machine in the post office: it absorbs the craft and skill associated with diagnosing telephone problems, robbing the craftsperson of both knowledge and technical skills.

In the United States, computerized equipment is used to test main trunk lines and to test lines and switching equipment when there are customer complaints. In the latter case, the equipment performs most of the tests automatically, reducing the work of the test-desk operator, one of the most skilled craft positions in the telecommunications industry, by roughly 60 percent. The trunk-line testing equipment, in use since 1980, increases line-testing productivity by 25 percent while reducing skills needed.

While jobs in manufacturing, installing and maintaining telephone systems are being eliminated or deskilled, the potential for new and more exciting jobs exists in applying those telephone systems in delivering the services of the information society of the future.

Something's wrong with the videotex, Ralph. I just tried to pay the gas bill and instead we're booked first class to Venezuela on the 15th.

5

The Information Society

While computers replace people in a lot of areas, such as in running factories and offices, they also open up new options, not only for employment but for new patterns of work and living. In fact, a dynamic world of new activity lies beyond the automation of traditional mechanical-age work, requiring only the right conditions to get it going. These include a favourable economic climate and people trained and able to exploit automated information and manufacturing systems in innovative new ways. A third condition is obviously the opportunity to do so.

The possibilities are suggested in existing innovations such as computer-aided instruction and medicine, computer chess and other electronic games, computer research services and computer conferencing. They're all aspects of what futurists regard as an emerging information society, or the "new information world order."

In their view, this society would feature an automated service-delivery system of which the automated office, the automated warehouse and the automated banking machine are but small pioneering pieces. When all the parts of the giant electronic jigsaw puzzle are in place, there would be computer terminals in homes as well as offices, in shopping malls, libraries and even gas stations, all speeding up and expanding our day-to-day activities. We would be transported from the relatively static world of print — forms, reports, blueprints, newspapers and books — into what has been called an intelligence universe. Its global network of computer communications systems would allow us to obtain information instantly, get in touch with other people, do business and see to our affairs for as long as we're plugged into this giant utility.

But how will this all come about? According to futurist Daniel Bell, the transition from an industrial to a postindustrial society will require a fundamental change in the way society uses information. Rather than playing a backup role, information must move forward to replace resources as the central axis around which other economic activity turns, and in so doing provide a new mainstay of employment. Employment in this new "information economy" won't come from traditional work in information handling and processing (which, of course, is being automated), but from applying information in making judgments or decisions or in creating something. In other words, the information society will employ creative knowledge workers, rather than information workers, or so the theory goes. Currently, many more people work as information workers than as knowledge workers.

As the delivery of services is automated and transformed into a self-serve activity, providing brokerage or information about services, advice and counselling, plus the creation and marketing of new services may become the new focal points of activity. Canadian banks are already stressing financial information services in their advertising.

Physically, the information society involves the integration of computers and several communications technologies: video, tape recorders, broadcast television, cable, telephones, records and even photography. By looking at three of the computer communications hybrids that could provide the architecture for the information society, we can get an idea of what this society might involve. As of 1981, they seemed quite dissimilar in their impact: while teletext is little more than a novel extension of existing media, and videodisc, while promising, is quite unproven, videotex is both a genuinely new medium and one that has obvious practical applications.

Videotex and Other Hydrids

Teletext displays computer-stored information on a television-like screen, either at home or in the office. There the viewer, using a small keypad, can freeze any frame in the ongoing parade and hold it on the screen for detailed reading. The information is broadcast, so the user can only select from what is being beamed across the information channel, just as a television viewer can only select from the offerings on different channels. In Britain, where both the ITV and the BBC television networks offer teletext information services, the more than 150,000 subscribers receive an assortment of news, sports and stock market reports. While it doesn't offer the range of choice of the more elaborate hybrids, teletext nevertheless does provide access to instantly updated computer-stored information. Being a relatively simple evolution of existing technology, teletext offers a minimal-risk stepping stone into the new information economy, although it sets a tone of its industries being more broadcast-oriented than truly interactive. In 1982, at least one Canadian company, Norpak, was offering limited teletext services, via cable television with a simple decoder attachment.

While teletext is close to mass media such as television and radio, videodisc involves both a greater degree of personal choice and the capability of *collecting* material. Thus it is more analogous to the world of books. In appearance, a videodisc is more like a device for storing a different sort of information: long-playing records. However, the videodisc has seventy-five times as many grooves per inch as the LP (it can store 3,200 books on just one side) and can hold information in a variety of forms: video, slides, print or voice. Users can build up a multimedia library of information and display it not just in the storage sequence, but in any order that happens to suit them. It's still too early to tell how videodisc will be used, as it's only just being introduced.

91

Videotex is among the more interesting hybrids, especially in Canada, where a homegrown version has been sponsored and promoted by the federal government — almost, it seems, as a deliberate strategy to hasten the advent of new employment opportunities by seeding the new information industrial activity. Like the telephone, videotex is a two-way (or interactive) information system; it can even be operated across phone lines. But there the similarity ends. Instead of a phone receiver, the user has a modified television set or a visual display terminal. And instead of a dial, the user has a keypad or, more likely since 1981, a typewriter-like keyboard. (A keypad comes with a separate modem adapter unit, while a keyboard has its modem built in.) Depending on what is keyed in, users can send for information already packaged (such as a newspaper column or set of statistics), search in data banks for other information, send and receive messages or conduct business affairs such as banking or mail-order-style shopping.

This livingroom manifestation of the computer revolution contains the same five basic components common to all computer systems. The keypad or keyboard is the input unit, while the output unit is either a television set or the visual display terminal of a word processing unit, computer terminal or microcomputer. The modem, or black box, contains the all-important processing unit for interpreting the user's demands and relaying the information back in videotex-page format. The memory function or unit can be a central storage unit, maintained by one of the companies providing information services on the videotex system. It might be a series of data banks in libraries, research institutes, corporate files. It might also be a personal library or electronic filing cabinet with the user storing information within the microcomputer or word processor or on videodiscs. The final component is the communications medium, which can be telephone lines or coaxial cables.

There are high hopes for videotex because it is versatile and easy to use — both for the person who creates the pages of material and for someone who's strictly an information consumer. The page creator's work is made easier thanks to the development of a simple information-formatting language. Canada's government-backed videotex system, Telidon (which was touted as the possible

North American standard in 1981), uses a language called picture description instructions (PDI). PDI allows computer-stored information to be displayed in print, graphs or even mosaic-like geometric pictures. The computerized version of the information is based on a limited alphabet of coded symbols: line, arc, rectangle and polygon (of up to 200 sides, which allows for fairly sophisticated drawings). Combinations of these codes are used to inscribe the most complex of images as videotex pages available on the user's terminal. Within the page creation system needed to do this work, a light pen or, more commonly, an electronic "mouse" functions as a pointer, telling the system's processor where, for instance, to start an arc or plot a graph. As the hand-held mouser unit is moved across an electronic workpad placed near the terminal, the motions are directly mirrored on the terminal screen.

But the user doesn't need to know the coding technique itself, only the simple method of operating the videotex system. This involves either following a series of either/or choices of direction arranged along a decision tree or calling up information according to a key index word (for the latter, of course, you have to know what keywords to punch in).

It's not just the knowledge of formatting language that separates the page creator from the noncreating consumer: there's quite a leap in price as well. While for the consumer, the basic equipment cost about $500 in 1981 (or as low as $150, for an adapter to turn a regular television set into a videotex terminal), a page-creation system typically cost $20,000. It would seem that the price gap could prevent videotex from becoming a truly interactive medium, turning it instead in the direction of existing mass media, with a few people producing and everyone else just consuming.

Even as a mass-market vehicle, videotex is still significant. Its simple formatting procedures effectively take computer-based information systems out of the corner of specialist control and put them into the nontechnical hands of the general public to be used in a host of service industries. This is why videotex could prove to be so important. It represents a possible bridge to the information society: just as Gutenberg's printing press helped to spread literacy, videotex, playing the same popularizing role, could speed computer literacy. However, the development of ever easier so-called high-level computer languages could whittle away any significant advantage the Telidon language might claim to offer.

New activity involving videotex could emerge on a number of fronts, including industries whose workers are being hardest hit by automation. Banks could package individualized videotex financial planning manuals or manage the videotex formatting of financial information, such as a comparison of interest rates on investments. Supermarkets could put together weekly menu suggestions according to criteria such as family size, budget constraints and special diet needs; and insurance companies could create self-help guides to selecting coverage. Telephone companies could serve as go-betweens or information brokers, providing access to computerized data banks.

The spread of videotex in business could also lead to the growth of a professions marketplace, where professionals such as accountants, lawyers and architects could advertise their services and send electronic mail ordering each other's self-serve software packages.

Another area with potential is small-business initiatives such as on-demand publishing, where a copy of a document is produced only when one is requested, sometimes as microfiche. There are at least two firms in this line of business in Canada. One company publishes the proceedings of scientific conferences in microfiche form, as requested by mail order. In future, the material could be ordered by electronic mail and transmitted that way as well, no doubt greatly increasing its appeal.

Videotex could also provide an electronic version of the town hall meeting, with citizens using their videotex terminals to signal their response in debates and opinion polls. It could also provide a forum for cultural exchange, with artists using the medium to generate and exchange poetry or perhaps computer art.

The possibilities are many but seem rather distant, given that in 1982 videotex in Canada was still a technology in waiting. In fact, it was a delivery system in search of something to deliver; there were few commercial videotex services available in Canada. Most activity was centred on manufacturing the system equipment, with a number of companies such as Norpak, Electrohome and Northern Telecom pressing on, convinced that once enough units were available, at a reasonable cost, videotex would take off just as television did in the 1950s.

Just as the first television programs were rather banal — essentially just radio with pictures — the first videotex services are rather prosaic as well. In Canada, they are little more than computerized versions of information found in newspapers. In the United States, the scope is only slightly larger; besides providing electronic newspaper files, they offer electronic forms of traditional consumer services. The department stores J.C. Penney and Sears Roebuck were offering teleshopping, where users key in their orders after perusing catalogue-like pages on their screens, and some American banks had experimented with using videotex for at-home banking.

In a Canadian development in teleshopping, Simpson-Sears mail-order customers in the Toronto area, at least those with push-button phones, can now place their orders on a self-serve basis by punching in the catalogue reference numbers on their phone key-pads. This development is thought to have had a bearing in Simpsons' trimming of 3,000 part-time jobs in Toronto shortly after this service was introduced in 1981.

Most Canadian applications of videotex are not in delivering services, however, but information. This is understandable given that a major pioneer in this new industry, Infomart, is a joint venture of two communications companies, Southam and Torstar. The two have invested $12 million in their new line of business and have developed a 40,000-page library of information.

Infomart's first commercial offering was the Grassroots service for prairie grain farmers. Introduced in 1981, Grassroots primarily provides special-interest information, such as weather conditions and up-to-the-minute grain prices. It has the potential for users to input their own material, although subscribers have not taken advantage of this possibility.

Also in 1981, Infomart launched a drive to install 2,000 terminals in Toronto for a new tourist information service called Teleguide. Installations are to include hotels, government offices and other public buildings. The pages of information range from a guide to restaurants (for hotels in Toronto) to bank-information services provided by the Bank of Montreal and real estate information indexed by location and price range and even including floor plans. By and large, the material is little more than electronic Yellow Pages or classified ads.

Infomart charges a flat subscription fee plus an amount for access time — a mere five cents per minute. One wonders whether it will remain that low when the service includes access to specialized research services; the Institute for Scientific Research in Philadelphia charges users up to $165 an hour to search through its reference material.

Industry enthusiasts predict that by 1985, half a million Canadian homes could have Telidon terminals, and that by 1990, there will be up to 40 million home subscribers to American videotex systems. These predictions are made in the face of estimates that world installations by 1981 were no more than 30,000, far fewer than the hundreds of thousands predicted for 1980–1981. Infomart had pared down its Teleguide terminal installation plans from 2,000 to 800, plus another 400 terminals which could be activated on a dial-up basis. And the British experience suggests that videotex does not have wide appeal among consumers: around 90 percent of the 15,000 subscribers to the Prestel service are businesspeople, not home users. The largest single user group is travel agents. And among home users, the most popular program is the daily horoscope, which hardly suggests a large scope for market growth.

At the least, this suggests that creating the information economy and unleashing its potential for fresh and more enriched employment might take longer than originally thought — longer than we have time for, before the current pace of automation makes such new employment essential to avoid mass unemployment. Perhaps the approach being taken is wrong; perhaps the premise that new information activities will emerge as naturally as the service sector emerged in the postwar period is wrong; perhaps the learner society or the knowledge society envisioned in the information society exists only in the imaginations of idealistic futurists. The experience to date in computer-aided instruction might provide some clues.

Computer-Aided Instruction

Computer-aided instruction (CAI) at its simplest involves the packaging of sequences of illustrations and instructions, with questions and answers to test comprehension along the way. Applications have included industrial training (operation of equipment and machinery, for instance), computer operation and standard academic subjects such as sciences, mathematics and languages.

This information industry is expected to boom during the 1980s, pushed by business, which in the United States is reportedly spending $30 billion a year on employee training and sees CAI as a means of restraining rising costs. Businessmen are encouraged by the claim of the Institute for Defense Analysis that computer-based systems have cut training time in the American armed forces by 30 percent and by the claim made to the World Conference of Banking Institutes in 1981 that CAI can cut corporate training times by 25 percent. As well, some of the more exotic applications of CAI — for example, in training the astronauts on the space shuttle program — have improved its popularity and credibility. (In preflight training for the Columbia, CAI was used to simulate the operation in space of the Canadian-made Canadarm robot arm.)

It appears that new developments will make CAI increasingly flexible throughout the 1980s. The use of videodiscs, in experiments such as those at the Ontario Institute for Studies in Education, seems promising in less disciplined subjects such as art appreciation, where a nonlinear format is required and can best be exploited. More important, though, are advances in programming languages that make them more "portable" — that is, applicable on a variety of computer systems — and able to handle auxiliary functions such as filing and recordkeeping. Most important, the new languages are easier to use so teachers can create course materials themselves without having to acquire programming skills or depend on a computer programmer. In some cases in the past, CAI software programs, called courseware, that were created by programmers alone were found to be deficient from an educational viewpoint. As well, the new programming languages make for more flexible, individualized instruction.

Just as poor-quality CAI software or courseware can actually hinder the learning process, so can CAI itself, if used inappropriately. The cost-cutting preoccupations inherent in industry's interest in CAI might pervade government and school-board thinking, downgrading the priority of providing the best possible education for the next generation. Instead of freeing teachers from rote teaching tasks to tutor and counsel students on a one-to-one basis, CAI might be used to replace teachers either directly or indirectly by increasing student–teacher ratios.

Financial considerations could also produce inequalities in education. Applications of the new, more flexible programming languages such as NATAL cost more than CAI developed earlier; hence some schools, whether they are driven to CAI by cost factors or not, might only be able to afford lower-quality options. As it is, private schools in Ontario were almost ten years ahead of public schools in installing computers as instructional aids and work tools.

This problem is much like the one of the steep fees being charged for data-base searches by institutes and libraries, whose services were intended to be free. If public libraries — whose services are customarily free, in the tradition of democratic ideals — turn toward electronic data bases as the major source of research information for the public, the search fee charged could restrict knowledge to an elite or at least impose a severe handicap on those who have to rely only on standard free-access print materials on library shelves.

Unless safeguards are put in place, the computer age, at least for a while, could resurrect some of the class barriers that liberal reformers spent much of this century trying to tear down. Already there is a distinct class-like advantage to being computer-literate.

There is also the issue of Canadian content. While major American textbook publishers are developing their own lines of courseware, and electronic giants such as Control Data and Texas Instruments are producing computer-learning products, there is little activity on the Canadian front. So the face of the computer learning business could end up the same as that of textbook publishing: mainly nonCanadian, in both ownership and content.

There are yet other concerns, arising from other areas of computer innovation. For instance, in computer-aided medicine, a diagnostic robot used in an Edinburgh, Scotland, hospital has proven more effective than some doctors. The robot has been programmed to be sympathetic as well as methodical. When the robot asks how long the pain has been going on and the patient replies, "Four weeks," the robot responds, "I'm sorry to hear that." When the robot asks how much a person with a history of alcohol problems drinks on average each day, the person doesn't feel embarrassed to tell the truth. The hospital has found that people will confess to drinking 30 percent more than they've told their doctors.

The situation begs the question, Who controls how these computer aids will be used? Will they do away with or enhance a doctor's diagnosis? Does the doctor control these decisions, or do hospital administrators and cost-conscious bureaucrats?

Control over the technology is crucial to how the information society is shaped. Will it be an open, participatory society with individuals able to use its operating tools and systems to do more and do better? Or will it be a society where most people are passive consumers of information goods and services supplied by a few who alone use its tools and systems? How many people are employed and how fully they are employed in the information economy will depend in part on how centralized the control is, whether it stays in Canada and how much initiative the individual can exercise. It's important to trace that control now, as companies building videotex delivery systems place themselves in strategic positions of influence within the unfolding information society.

The Owners of the Technology

In both the United States and Canada, it appears that powerful companies in the communications and media field are becoming major players in the videotex field.

The most dramatic American example is the joint videotex venture being negotiated between CBS — with $2 billion in assets, one of the largest communications and media companies in the United States — and AT&T — with $125 billion in assets, considered the world's largest company. The plan, announced in 1981, is to bring videotex services into the 80 percent of American homes that AT&T already supplies with telephones. Besides its broadcast holdings, CBS publishes textbooks and sixty magazines. So the joint venture has both a means to deliver information and a base of information to work from. Its edge in these two roles — carrier and content — means the CBS–AT&T project has a large competitive advantage over other would-be contenders in the videotex industry. The same is true of another joint venture involving AT&T, in which the phone giant and the Knight-Ridder newspaper chain, one of the largest in the United States, will supply Florida homes with shopping guides and educational material packaged by the newspaper company.

Infomart, Canada's foremost player in the videotex industry, also has the advantage of embodying both the carrier and content roles. As well, the parties involved have an added benefit in their built-in information resource base. Torstar owns the country's largest daily, the *Toronto Star*, as well as book and magazine publishing operations and a large chain of weeklies. Southam controls a third of the English-language daily newspaper market in Canada, controls numerous business publications and indirectly controls several radio and television stations.

The enormous power that the integration of carrier and content roles bestows can be seen in other media in Canada. Telephone companies are a prime example of the single role of communications carrier; they tend to enjoy steady but not spectacular earnings. Book publishers play an exclusively content role; they tend to have a feast-or-famine existence, with their survival in constant peril for lack of the steady income that is typical of carrier service.

However, companies that charge for playing both roles, providing content as well as the carriage delivery service, fare the best; they enjoy steady and generally high earnings. Examples include movie chains, which often own the theatres showing their films, and newspapers. Bell Canada seems to have learned this truth: its Vista system is Infomart's main rival in the Canadian videotex industry.

Those who have tried to have Canadian-made films shown in the chain-owned cinemas can attest to how vital access to the carrier system is to economic viability of the content — the Canadian film industry. Producers find it difficult to get their films distributed.

The film industry offers another lesson as well. When the motion-picture camera was invented, there were lofty predictions of everyone being able to direct their own films, rather like current futurists' predictions that everyone will participate in the open "knowledge," "learner" or "information" society. Although the Super-8 camera now makes popular participation possible on a hobby basis, the development of the mega-dollar film and the mega-dollar film industry soon restricted the original vision of filmmaking to control by a mere handful.

The pattern is repeated throughout history. Even in the most venerable of activities, farming, the high cost and technical sophistication of modern farm equipment have restricted access to an ever-diminishing handful of agribusinessmen.

Would-be providers of information products and services through Canada's videotex system may experience the same restrictions, with decisive implications for the scope of participation as producers, not just consumers in the information society. These restrictions may even be unintentional. For instance, the fee charged for making information available on a videotex system might escalate with rising equipment purchases and then reach a point where only material with mass-market appeal is left. It is very significant that there already exists such a large difference in cost to become a producer, versus a consumer, of videotex information services.

As well, the large companies such as Infomart have already gained a significant leverage over any would-be newcomers to the industry, including those interested in turning the electronic information delivery system or "intelligence universe" into an open information exchange, rather like the feudal market square.

These companies can set a mass-production standard of operation which would become imperative because of the costliness of the operating equipment they develop. They can also subsidize their operations through the use of information and equipment already paid for in related corporate ventures — newspapers in the case of Infomart.

Financial and other assistance to enfranchise a diversity of participants in videotex and other information industries—through the federal government's industrial-development aid program, for instance—might be useful. The government should perhaps also provide a public videotex delivery system, or at least ensure that minority information interests and tastes are served as well as the mass-market ones.

Theoretically, of course, anyone can become an information provider or provide the content to be packaged by someone like Infomart who has the costly page-creation equipment. Then you merely negotiate for storage space and access to audiences with Infomart, which owns the host computer. In practice, though, there is a danger of restrictive access inherent in control over the host computer, a control that is no less real for being invisible. Infomart, which supplies the carrier system and also packages the information content, decides what is suitable for the target audience of that information package — farmers, in the case of the Grassroots service. In the absence of regulations, members of the videotex industry, through their industry association, VISPAC, have prepared a code of ethics that states as one of its eleven points, "Information providers and system operators will not oppose the principle of freedom to participate in the videotex industry of any other existing or potential information provider."

The statement lacks the force of law; still, in the absence of a legal framework for videotex, it at least acknowledges the danger of restricting the sources of information — a danger that is nonetheless aggravated by the carrier and content roles (including content packager) being filled by one company.

This danger in the emerging field of electronic publishing was of some concern to the Kent Royal Commission on Newspapers. The commission was set up by the federal government in 1981 after the infamous wave of newspaper closings by Southam and another communications giant, Thomson. Its mandate was to explore the effect of corporate concentration on the freedom and diversity of information available in a society. (In the course of the commission's hearings, Torstar eliminated competition for its chain of weekly papers in suburban Toronto and outlying markets by buying the rival Inland chain.)

In addition to condemning the extreme concentration of ownership in the newspaper industry as being contrary to the public interest, the Kent commission expressed concern that ownership and control of electronic publishing might become similarly concentrated. It warned, "Removing the wall of separation between content and carrier . . . would favour the development of monopoly information services . . ." Furthermore, it said, under such a system, "freedom of the press as defined for centuries would be extinguished almost by accident."

Concentration of ownership in the media is not restricted to newspapers and videotex. A 1975 study found that media groups also controlled a majority of cable television systems (53 percent, accounting for 77 percent of the overall revenue), private radio stations (80 percent) and private television stations (56 percent). Yet the federal government appears indifferent to the problem of the carrier and content roles in large media both falling into the same hands, and the hands of already large media groups at that.

One problem that could arise, given the performance of privately owned Canadian television and radio stations in the past, is a lack of Canadian content. But as of 1981 there were no plans to run a public videotex system as an alternative vehicle for Canadian content, nor was the Canadian Radio-television and Telecommunications Commission exploring, let alone designing, a regulatory framework that would address the issue of Canadian content (or, indeed, the carrier–content separation recommended by the Kent commission).

As international business becomes increasingly plugged in to the expanding electronic information network, other peculiarly Canadian aspects of the ownership and content issue will likely arise. One of the most difficult aspects is, of course, foreign ownership and control of Canadian industry. Canadian subsidiaries are vulnerable to a further truncation of autonomy as parent companies exploit the potential for centralizing their information work — a potential that is greatly enhanced by using services such as a new joint venture involving IBM called Satellite Business Systems (SBS). Offering a range of information services through a worldwide communications grid, SBS features facsimile transmission (in which information expressed as printed words or even photographs is digitized and decoded back into the original print-paper form at the receiving end) and audio and video teleconferencing, as well as all forms of data transmission. IBM reportedly hopes that the SBS system will reduce the cost of transmitting information to something approaching insignificance, which will, of course, help companies interested in centralizing their data processing. Traditionally, high transmission costs encouraged companies to leave this work where the data itself is generated — within Canadian subsidiary operations, for instance. Enough transborder data flow was going on through conventional communications links well before the SBS development, however, that it was considered an issue with implications for Canadian sovereignty as well as for jobs. A study commissioned by the federal Department of Communications in the late 1970s concluded that at the rate data processing work was being transferred south of the border, the lost business could add $1.5 billion to Canada's current-account deficit by 1985 and relocate 23,000 jobs in data processing from Canada into the United States. A conference reviewing this study was told that the total could be as high as 100,000 jobs lost if professional and management jobs associated with applying the results of the data processing were included.

Consider the implications of an American-owned energy company relaying the raw results of exploration tests to its head-office computer department for processing, then to analysts there who would draw conclusions about available reserves and the probable cost of extracting them. Besides the erosion of autonomy in the Canadian subsidiary company, Canada would be deprived of this vital information on Canadian energy resources.

Yet after an initial flurry of concern, the federal government became strangely silent on the transborder data flow issue, perhaps in unspoken acceptance of Canada's impotence on the matter. These questions and issues remain, however, and demand public attention.

Perhaps the most crucial of all is the employment question — how to ensure that the information society grows fast enough and in a manner that will provide employment for Canadians as traditional jobs in industry and in information handling are automated.

Perhaps the laissez-faire approach won't be enough, for the private sector is bound to conservative investment, and the immediate-return perspective in which the private sector operates is not the best one for encouraging the growth of brand-new industries. Yet the federal government has set aside only $1 million of the Telidon industrial development program for projects run by non-profit groups. Unlocking the demand for information as an end in itself, creating new applications of information that will whet that demand, training people as page creators — these are as important as helping to install the equipment of the information society. Without these other issues being addressed, videotex could remain stuck in the status it was assigned by its critics and skeptics in 1982: a technology in search of an application.

Aside from the economic and cultural issues, more political or philosophical issues, such as the defence of privacy, must also be addressed. Already employees in a variety of lines of work are being monitored by computer, and there is a possibility that electronic eavesdropping could be extended to people's personal lives. A daily record of someone using videotex for banking, tele-shopping, electronic mail and research would provide an insightful profile: who you know, what you say to them, what you buy, your debts, your reading habits, your association memberships and so on. The idea of Big Brother spying may indeed seem preposterous. But it's worth remembering that police forces in Canada don't hesitate to make regular use of electronic surveillance, legally or otherwise, and that it was revealed in 1981 that the list of people the RCMP considered to be possible security risks ran to more than half a million names.

The rise of computer crime has shown that the electronic world is not impervious to snoopers of one kind or other. Students at an exclusive private school in New York state used the school computer terminals to penetrate the computerized files of twenty-one Canadian companies during the spring of 1980, managing to erase one-fifth of the information in one company's system. The incredible part of this caper wasn't so much that it could be so easily done, but that the students had committed no crime. There still is no criminal legislation directly related to computer-stored information.

There are many fronts, then, on which the new technology will affect Canadians as individuals and as a nation. The next chapter looks at one response — heading for occupations that are likely to grow in a computer-oriented working world — and how the reorganization of work can itself be a means of fostering new employment opportunities.

Hi, we're the Andersons, and we've just become computer literate. Do you want to interface?

6

New Jobs
and Career Paths

You don't have to become a computer scientist or engineer to survive the microchip revolution and find employment in the office, the factory or the information industries of the future. It's true that there is and will continue to be a crisis-level demand for engineers, computer scientists and technologists to create and implement new computer systems. For example, Canadian industry is expected to need 45,000 new engineers and applied scientists between 1979 and 1985 alone, some 15,000 more than our universities are thought able to train.

However, *applying* these systems will require people who can straddle the computer world and traditional lines of work. In other words, familiarity with computers will become part of the basic core of competence, like the abilities of planning, communicating and so on. This basic computer literacy includes logic and analytical skills associated with mathematics and a general understanding of how computer systems work. In different lines of innovative new work, of course, various computer skills may be called for as well.

In the frontier stages of this application phase, it's not surprising to find a lot of employment occurring in small companies that spring up to market new computer innovations. Current examples include firms selling computer-controlled security systems, data bank services, blueprints for installing office-of-the-future systems and even computer dating. There's also a company in Toronto, called Compu-Palm, that offers computer-aided fortune telling. These ventures — most of them, anyway — require skills and knowledge in other fields as well as in computers and engineering. For instance, a company selling data bank or videotex services to companies with the automated information systems to receive them will need people with backgrounds in graphic art (for creating videotex pages) and library science (to know how to structure and index the data bank) in addition to computer literacy and an understanding of computer systems and some computer skills. The same duality is found in information industries such as computer-aided instruction and electronic games.

Most employment in the long run will probably derive from a third source: work in traditional industries that has been enhanced, enriched or otherwise transformed. The office administrator will increasingly require computer literacy and some programming skills in managing the resources of automated information systems, and support staff will require technical skills to maintain the computer and communications equipment. The evolutionary approach to new employment opportunities is already apparent in the banks, where tellers are being renamed customer service representatives as they spend more time advising customers on services that the banks offer — and that are increasingly being delivered automatically. Similarly, telephone operators could evolve to become information brokers, putting customers in touch with data retrieval and research services around the world.

Some confusing job titles could result during the transition to a computer-assisted work world. For instance, someone hired out of the computer science field to run the computerized reference services of an automated library might be called an applications engineer. However, if the reference librarian acquired computer programming skills and information systems knowledge to complement his or her library science education and experience, such a person would probably still be called a reference librarian. Of course, none of these professions is likely to evolve from a minor group of workers to a major one, as significant as tellers and secretaries, unless information attains a greater status.

Whether new jobs will result from evolution or from replacing redundant personnel in traditional work with new recruits also depends on other factors, such as personnel policies among employers. Providing opportunities for training and retraining as well as for occupational bridging and job redesign is obviously conducive to evolution.

For the moment, this chapter concentrates on specific employment developments anticipated over the next ten to fifteen years. The survey begins with the implementer occupations: the engineers, computer scientists and related technical staff who are installing computer systems throughout Canadian industry. Next, a review of jobs in videotex, an example of an innovative new industry; and third, transformations of traditional jobs will be examined.

Computer Science Occupations

There are essentially three types of computer professionals. Those in computer systems, such as systems analysts and designers, devise the overall requirements of a computer communications system. Second, people involved in hardware put together the physical framework for the system and designate where the nuts and bolts of the component parts should go. And third, software specialists work out the internal operating roles of the computer system and the programs for running various work projects through them.

The hierarchy includes engineers with different backgrounds — some specializing in communications devices, for instance, others in electronic switching systems. They design and construct the lowest-cost, most efficient physical operating unit for making the systems analyst's ideas work. They usually work with the systems analyst and computer specialists from the beginning.

While most of the design and development work is done by the

111

computer and engineering professionals — all with at least one university degree and usually several years' experience — the college-trained technologists actually implement the system. In addition, a number of technical support people, such as computer operators and electronics technicians, are involved.

A look at some jobs within these broad categories follows — it should be remembered, however, that responsibilities for each occupation vary considerably from industry to industry and from company to company; indeed, in the still-evolving world of computers there is no fixed universal set of job descriptions, and there is a lot of overlapping between occupations.

Computer Systems

Systems Analyst: This most senior person in the computer science occupational hierarchy works within the larger corporate system as a specialized corporate planner and as an intermediary between the corporation and its computer centre. The analyst identifies the problemsolving needs the computer system can meet and designs a master plan of computer subsystem strategies and tasks to achieve those larger goals. Someone at this level would typically have at least one degree in engineering, mathematics or computer science and extensive business experience.

Systems Designer: This person, whose work picks up where the system analyst's leaves off, translates the functional specifications of the computer system into operational specifications. In other words, the designer takes the specifications on what is needed and figures out how to achieve it—for instance, with a certain combination of electronic switching equipment and communications lines. He or she then assigns each specified subtask to the various computer experts in the department, mostly programmers and hardware and software specialists, to integrate the program into the company's expanding computer communications system. This person, who could also be called a project manager, also sees to it that the work follows the systems analyst's basic blueprint. Again, a number of backgrounds are possible: statistics, computer science or technical engineering. The designer might even have a degree in systems engineering — unique in Canada to the University of Waterloo.

Systems Implementer: This person, who could also be called a project engineer, oversees the actual implementation of the computer communications system. If training, staff reorganization or additional personnel are required, he or she will be the one to coordinate these needs with the personnel department. As well, the systems implementer must coordinate equipment purchases within the company's budget constraints. A detailed timetable must be established and adhered to and, finally, a report prepared.

Computer Science Technologist: The technologist, holding a diploma after a two- or three-year course of practical study at a community college or polytechnic, helps put the systems together. This might include pricing the best computer peripherals and arranging for data telecommunications links.

Systems Maintenance Person: Although the title suggests repair work, the responsibilities can range from planning and scheduling various projects through the company's computer system to assigning technical and clerical personnel who will test performance standards and specifying changes in user manuals and computerized instructional material. The job could become an important training ground for senior clerical–technical staff.

Computer Operator: Such persons, equivalent in skill to clerical workers or factory machine operators, are already in decreasing relative demand as computer systems become increasingly simplified and responsive to remote control. Still, people are needed to shunt work projects through the computer system, to mount, remove and store computer tapes where these are needed, and coordinate work between user groups — word and data processor operators, branch personnel, and so forth. This would be another good training ground for gaining some on-the-job computer literacy.

Like the systems maintenance person, the computer operator is an example of support jobs that come into the picture when the automated information system has been installed. Most support staff can be expected to have a technical background, which they could acquire through certificate or diploma programs at community college. These programs, often one year long, should cover basic electronics, digital equipment, computer languages and structures.

113

Software

Programmer: This professional computer worker acts as the go-between, translating the requirements of the problemsolving project outlined by the systems designer or systems analyst into ever more defined subproblems and finally into a program that can be run on a computer. After all, a program is simply a set of instructions, like those for assembling a bookcase or knitting a sweater. The job can be broken into its components, and in fact it is often broken down in order to provide a hierarchy of programmer occupations, ranging from the professional to the clerical level. A programmer has a math degree or is a community college graduate; a senior programmer has some experience.

Computer Science Technologist: This community college graduate, who has specialized in computer languages, actually does the craft-work of writing the computer program, working from a set of precise descriptions that the senior programmer has set down.

Maintenance: There is clerical work associated with software development just as there is in the running of total computer systems. A major part of this work is updating and making modifications to the program. For every quirk and nuance of the software program being developed, there is a clerical task in documenting that quirk in a guide for future users of the program; such user manuals require precise language and a disciplined approach. They're also constantly revised; every time the program bumps ("crashes") into some unforeseen outcome of the computations, the software is updated, revised, modified or repaired accordingly and duly documented. All of this is considered maintenance work.

Software Assistant: This clerical job, also considered part of data processing, involves gathering information required in writing software and documenting the software steps onto worksheets. As for software maintenance, this technical job requires a year or two of study at community college.

Data Encoder: This is another position in support work, although more professional in nature. It requires an aptitude if not for computer languages, at least for language itself and, within that, for indexing. The encoder stands at the threshold between the computer and the real world, devising the boxes into which that real world must be coded or digitized for the information to be processed by a computer. This classification work, as well as the original work of devising the most appropriate multiple-choice pigeonholes into which the information is classified, requires a good grasp of taxonomy — the principles of classification — as well as of programming.

Hardware

While the systems people devise the overall computer systems environment and software people develop the internal operating rules and procedures on which these systems run, the hardware people put together the framework and the operating machinery that make the whole system work.

Engineers: An engineer designs computer systems and their component parts. Mechanical engineers are found more in automated factories than in offices and information industries. In these latter settings, a host of electrical engineers are found, specializing in communications systems, control systems, electronics circuits or perhaps electrical transmission systems.

Depending on the task at hand, other specialists might also be involved, forming an interdisciplinary design and development team. Increasingly, computer scientists and electronics engineers are teaming up, especially in the production of firmware, where the operating software is built into the hardware; a pocket calculator is an example.

Technologist: The computer equivalent of skilled tradespeople, technologists implement the hardware systems designed by the engineers. While engineers have a university education, technologists are community college graduates. They actually put together the circuit-board hardware designed by engineers and ferry the product through the testing stage. Then, working with programmers and clerical maintenance personnel, they help draft the operating specifications and prepare the operating manual and, usually, the operator's self-instruction program that accompanies the completed hardware.

Maintenance Technician: These personnel would range from those with clerical and writing skills for preparing the user-instruction material to field-staff technicians who would actually install the new equipment and serve as trouble-shooters.

115

Videotex Occupations

There are three categories of work in this pioneer information systems industry: developing the technology (hardware and software) associated with videotex systems; developing the content of videotex information systems; and packaging, installing, marketing and promoting videotex systems and services. The latter two areas could provide large-scale employment in a variety of occupations. Many of these jobs were described in Chapter 5.

Most of the research and development has been performed in the Ottawa area, both in government and in the new high-technology companies. Jobs in the other two categories are largely confined to the Toronto area. Assuming videotex continues to grow as an industry, however, there could soon be considerable employment in these two occupation groups across Canada.

Technology Development

Telidon was developed during ten years of intensive laboratory research work sponsored by the federal Department of Communications. It will continue to evolve with developments in telecommunications technology. As well, electrical and other engineers will be needed to develop units for translating Telidon signals so they can be handled on regular television sets, home and office computers and word processing terminals. Expanding the scope and versatility of Telidon packaging, computer specialists will refine the text creation language to make it increasingly easy for noncomputer types to use. They will also improve the cross-referencing software for more versatile data bank research. Unfortunately, not many people will be needed for this research and development, handfuls at most.

Information Providers

Some of the most promising and diversified work associated with videotex services will lie in developing their information content. In the short term, the content will include existing material in newspapers and magazines, corporate policy and operations information intended for in-house training and government service information, for business as well as home videotex audiences.

Examples would be step-by-step tax guides for small businesses and homeowners, and information on government assistance to small business, single parents and senior citizens, including guidelines on how to apply.

Possible source of information are as plentiful as the possible applications. One source could be the individual teacher who produces Telidon material — maps, diagrams, pictorials — for correspondence students, incorporating an electronic mail feature for transmitting assignments and for remote tutoring. With a Telidon page-creation machine, requiring little technical knowledge to use, almost anyone with interesting or useful information could become an information provider — that is, assuming the system's structure and the surrounding policy and regulatory infrastructure allows and favours this diverse participation, and leaving aside the cost factor.

As the example of the teacher suggests, content-development work won't necessarily be done in videotex companies themselves but in organizations already dealing in information that are taking advantage of the new medium. There are three basic occupations involved in developing this information content: page creators, editors and systems designers.

Page Creators: Creating pages on videotex systems involves text-display work, akin to what a traditional secretary or copy editor does. The page creator needs the ability to write clearly and a sense of graphics and illustration, applied to the picture description instructions alphabet (in the case of Telidon) for geometric image-making. Given the amount of shared ground with existing media, it is not surprising that page creators typically come from backgrounds in newspapers, ad agencies and animation work, as well as in data processing.

Editor: This occupation involves structuring information packages for use on videotex systems. The editor will act as a coordinator when information packages are being created for a specific user group. For instance, a bank might want to transform in-house policy information currently in bulky personnel manuals into Telidon packages that not only could be readily pulled up onto a user's terminal screen but also could be quickly updated. The editor, acting as a project manager, would work with the bank's

117

personnel to design the most appropriate structuring mechanism for both the information and the anticipated use situation. Videotex editing is an obvious opening for print writers and editors who are eager to catch the wave of the new technology.

Systems Designer: The key to successful Telidon videotex systems is how well they're structured: either according to keyword indexes or along a decision tree of algorithmic either/or choices. This requires an understanding of how people learn and pursue information as well as a basic understanding of computer programming. People working here have backgrounds in library science and skills in taxonomy and indexing. The specific information packages also have to be incorporated into the generic indexes and introduction menus (like tables of contents) of the videotex information service as a whole. Users flipping through the menu on their home videotex systems might key in for a more detailed index or menu under the initial entry "entertainment." This menu might provide a further subset of choices — for instance, the category "electronic games" leading to a choice between educational, science fiction, sports-related or other types of games, and so on.

At a more sophisticated level, a systems designer will work with data bank librarians to build gateway or mediator features, so that users can reach through videotex services to the most detailed research material in the most remote of data banks.

Marketing and Distribution

This line of work is a good prospect for someone interested in marketing, advertising or sales, or for those already in such careers. Terminal and converter vendors will sell the service in the same way that cable services are marketed. Videotex consultants will likely work with industries to develop Telidon information packages based on in-house information or material obtainable elsewhere, and they will advise on how to exploit the technology still further — possibly by contributing the in-house information packages to a public videotex service. Private companies may market the information packages they've developed, such as electronic magazines, or packages obtained on a franchise basis, data banks and data research services, for example. This activity touches on the potential in distributing videotex services, not just creating them. An example would be financial consultative services and information packages created by or in conjunction with Canadian banks, or information on the Arctic, on oceanography and on resource exploration, which, being areas of Canadian expertise, could conceivably become the basis for commercial data bases here. These might be sold to or traded with videotex systems in other countries.

New Directions for Traditional Jobs

From the evidence of previous chapters, it's obvious that traditional office and factory work has passed its zenith as a source of employment. By way of a review, these are the characteristics of jobs that are likely to be automated if they haven't yet been.
- Repetitive work without decisionmaking responsibility
- Support work rather than work exercising control and initiative
- Work consisting of reporting and recording
- Monitoring, supervising, orchestrating procedures and scheduling work and people
- Work where judgment has been replaced by reliance on logic and statistical analysis

There are measures that people finding themselves in about-to-be-automated jobs can take to protect themselves against layoffs and to prepare for, and ensure, their mobility to new areas of work; these are discussed in the next two chapters. But action is also needed by employers, not only to ensure that they have the human resources necessary to design and launch innovative applications of computer technology but also to help avoid the terrible social problems associated with widespread unemployment.

Support Staff

In a research study by Xerox, designed to win converts to electronic information systems, secretaries were given free rein to exploit the full computer communications power available through word processing units. The results demonstrated that office automation need not lead to unemployment, but can open up a range of new career paths. At first the secretaries in the project experimented with off-the-shelf software for tasks such as checking spelling and mailing-list work. Eventually, many got tired of the limitations of these features and learned programming on their own. One secretary also took courses in computer-aided graphics and graduated from simply typing correspondence to preparing large reports. This is one potential career path: into text processing, including formatting and graphic illustration.

Given the opportunity, clerical workers could move ahead with the new technology on many fronts. That opportunity involves a new approach to the organization of work, one featuring an ongoing evolution of job functions so that as automation absorbs one function, only the related skills become redundant. This approach presupposes ongoing or continuing education and training as well, so that, for instance, as traditional teller skills are taken over by automation, bank workers can move into new job functions applying new computer-related skills. Ideally all jobs should be multifunctional — consisting of several tasks and functions. This would allow the inclusion of a learning and training component and would lend itself to occupational mobility. Thus, automation could lead to simply the redundancy of some functions (and their replacement with new functions) rather than the redundancy of people.

Such a strategy is essential to help women workers in particular, to overcome occupational segregation and the traditions that give rise to it. Sometimes called occupational bridging, the strategy would involve deliberately designing opportunities for growth and mobility into work situations that have traditionally left women trapped in single-function support occupations. In the United States, these affirmative action measures have taken the form of legal obligations (called consent decrees) imposed on companies found to be in violation of equal opportunity legislation. They've proven quite effective. In one case, the giant telephone utility AT&T signed a consent decree in 1973. By its expiry in 1979, women had doubled their representation in middle- and upper-management positions to 18 percent of all such positions, had nearly doubled their representation in the sales force, to 45 percent, and had tripled their representation in inside craft jobs, to 18 percent of these jobs. Interestingly, the vice-chairman of the board at

AT&T has acknowledged that such changes would not have been made if they hadn't been mandatory. In Canada, by comparison, where women as a group still earn less than 60 percent of what men earn, and where affirmative action has not been mandatory, progress has been negligible. Yet such strategies are essential today, not only as a women's right but for the benefit of the larger economy — to help avoid skills gaps and skills shortages that, in turn, could jeopardize the innovation phase of applying automated information and manufacturing systems.

The work path described earlier is but one direction in which traditional support staff can go; it would be appropriate for someone interested in public relations work or possibly in personnel, preparing in-house courseware for training. Other directions might be data-file formatting for data network and information management; computer-aided research for policy decisionmaking in the executive ranks; and data processing for accounting and business administration. Some extra education would probably be essential as well as introductory computer courses for basic computer literacy; but this education could be combined with on-the-job experience, possibly in training or co-op work-study programs.

One key to continuous employment is through organizing the work and designing job descriptions in a way that facilitates growth and job mobility.

A career path in data-bank management might begin with a job reorganization, from simply filing paper correspondence and the like to encoding material to be fed into the electronic filing system and later working with a computer specialist to refine the coding system to better fit the particular information milieu. More demanding work to follow might involve identifying the cross-references needed in the software running the data network to fit more effectively with the company's information needs and uses and, as a next step, actually making those modifications to the software. With experience, and possibly some outside study in library science and administration, one could go on to more taxing work, being responsible for more aspects of the data base and its overall design and administration, and finally moving into middle management.

As data bases grow, so too will career possibilities in managing them. And as the value of effectively accessing and exploiting those data bases continues to parallel that growth, so the work of information brokerage will develop as a career as well.

One aspect of this work could become a new source of employment for displaced telephone operators. This would involve connecting customers to the commercial data bases proliferating across North America. The work would require keeping up to date on these data bases, knowing their access protocols (call numbers really) and perhaps also advising customers on what data base would best suit their needs.

Someone working as an information broker within an office setting would probably also get involved in actually conducting the keyword searches and compiling the research information. A first stepping stone out of simple paper-file retrieval might involve simply expediting keyword searches where the research approach has already been drafted by a more experienced person. On developing research skills on the job and possibly after some outside study in library reference and archival work, this junior information broker could move on to conducting the whole information search and retrieval project herself. At a more senior level, she might act as a paraprofessional resource contact person for the senior professional–managerial group.

Information brokerage and research work promises to provide enough challenge and variety for a career in itself, assuming that information continues to grow in value. The work could also lead laterally into information packaging, to personnel and public relations work, or into information analysis — such as market and financial analysis — for decisionmaking.

Someone aspiring to the executive ranks either in marketing or in corporate planning and financial management might steer toward research work as an assistant to such an executive. The work would require enough familiarity with the computer system to call up material from data files and to process it using simple techniques of statistical analysis — percentage difference, standard deviation and so forth — to yield decisionmaking insights. A former secretary might key in search-and-sort instructions to have all the customer-complaint correspondence polled according to different key words and phrases. Having obtained this data, the budding market analyst might key in instructions to analyze the relative frequency of complaints about, say, package design and construction as contrasted with package instructions, and conclude with a strong case for changing the packaging material because it's too hard to tear. Again, night courses in marketing and business administration would round out the prospects for mobility.

Courses in accounting and business administration would help someone moving from strictly data-base management into office-systems administration. An administrative assistant with a good knowledge of how the office works can help a newly hired computer programmer to tailor software for the management information system to best meet the organization's needs. After taking some computer courses, including programming languages and principles, to supplement the knowledge gained from working with the programming specialist, the assistant could move on to doing this work himself or herself, as a computer-literate office systems administrator. Research has found, incidentally, that it's more cost-effective to retrain staff to work with a computerized system (as opposed to a traditional manual or mechanized system) than it is to replace traditional staff with computer experts who understand the new technology but require costly education before they can apply it effectively within a particular office or factory operation.

Entry-level support staff, too, will require more skills and generally more technical ones than they used to. With the increasing proliferation of electronic office equipment — word processors, electronic information switching equipment, computers of all kinds — the need for people to run, care for and diagnose the problems of this equipment and repair it will also grow. Community college courses in basic electronics, automated office systems and equipment would be obvious preparation for work in the offices of the future.

Management
Traditional office administration is being transformed into computer-assisted administration. Middle managers of the future will work more with computer programs and systems than with forms and manuals. As the automation of reporting also removes the

need for strict reporting hierarchies, a much looser, more open management style becomes possible. In fact, some analysts predict this new style will emphasize more self-management, which could make some alternative working arrangements more popular, in an overall concern for improving the quality of working life. The electronic cottage or telecommuting concept, which involves working from a computer terminal at home, is one of the alternatives; flexible working hours, or flextime, is another.

No longer managing people, the middle manager of the future is likely to be more of a facilitator or resource person, putting the resources of the computer communications system to work most effectively for the professionals and senior executives. This person won't need to become a computer programmer or systems analyst, but will need computer literacy and some skills in designing and running computer systems. Given the right opportunities to evolve (educational leave, on-the-job training and job reorganization), the traditional office administrator could easily become a systems administrator in the office of the future. However, in 1981 at least, most systems people were computer scientists and engineers who had effectively superseded the work of traditional administrators.

These professionals are rising to senior corporate positions as well. But it's difficult to say whether computer professionals will turn out to be the new elite of business, much as industrial psychologists came to be perceived as indispensable to labour relations in the heyday of industrial psychology. The spread of computer literacy and the attitude that these professionals are "just computer specialists" could leave them in a more auxiliary role instead.

Blue-Collar Jobs
In industry, since the focus of new work is on information — designing the specifications of something that is then produced automatically — it is unrealistic to expect new employment to emerge within the factory setting itself. New employment will appear off the assembly and production floor, in the white-collar setting of offices and salesrooms. This might involve promoting and selling the products of automated manufacturing, and even creating such new information services as computer-aided manufacturing.

124

Although jobs in processing, parts assembly and materials handling are disappearing as automation enters factories, some new employment is being created. Instead of operating machines and handling materials, factory workers will tend, maintain and otherwise support the automated machines and manufacturing systems. They will be computer systems technologists and technicians rather than machinists. Their work would range from helping to implement automated manufacturing programs according to specifications laid out in the blueprints, to statistical programming for inventory control and maintaining and repairing the automated systems. A broad range of skills associated with metal fabrication, machine tool operation and mechanical and electrical systems is replaced with a fairly narrow band of largely electronic skills.

In the factory of the future, the craftsperson is replaced with computer and electronics technologists who can work with computer programming professionals to refine automated manufacturing systems, including the software for numerically controlled machine tools. Their knowledge of the subsystems, steps and component tasks of the manufacturing process complements the computer specialist's skill in fine-tuning the new automated manufacturing processes.

There will undoubtedly be a continuing demand for some middle-level skilled workers to build integrated manufacturing systems. These would include electricians, pipefitters, millwrights, metal workers and welders. The future for engineers, not only electrical and mechanical but industrial, civil and plant engineers as well, is undoubtedly bright, at least while they're needed to build the automated design and manufacturing systems. Given the opportunity to apply automated design and manufacturing systems as innovative tools once they've built them in the name of productivity and increased competitiveness, these professionals can help create the structures and foster the operating capacity for the new information industries to grow.

In the factory of the future, the work of foremen and supervisors is likely to become obsolete, and factory administrative staff will shift their attention from managing people to managing machinery and manufacturing information systems. The work would involve the same three basic areas as in the office of the future: systems

125

administration, essentially looking after various automated systems; systems design, developing new systems and applying them, using blue-collar technicians and technologists as assistants; and systems analysis, which involves extending the scope of the factory's computer communications systems and appliances, simplifying their operations and reducing their costs.

Jobs for Canadians

While the discussion in this chapter may imply that there will be lots of jobs in a variety of areas, for newcomers to the labour force as well as for those being displaced by office and factory automation, the pace of job creation that is truly new (as opposed to recycled) is not encouraging. Nor can corporations realistically be expected to embark on new risk ventures on the frontier of the information age when high interest rates make entrepreneurship an almost suicidal indulgence. Yet, without new employment growth, what will prevent the unemployment rate from rising to Depression-like levels? It has been estimated that with the automation potential currently available, all the existing goods and services of our society could be produced by a mere 10 percent of the labour force.

It is not surprising, then, that the federal government's job-sharing program has been so well received. A means of dividing diminishing workloads and thereby spreading the burden of unemployment, this program calls for individuals to work only part of a normal work week and to collect unemployment insurance for the remainder. Switching to part-time work is another strategy for sharing reduced work, although the accompanying lack of job security and benefits needs to be redressed.

To a certain extent, these are only stopgap measures; for economic growth in the long term, we need to develop a sound industrial base anchored in a strong electronics manufacturing capacity and supported by Canadian research and development. But in the short term, to fill the job shortfall that has become a classic feature of the transition between the implementation and matured innovation stages of introducing new technology, other employment strategies should be considered. These might include more statutory holidays, more paid educational and other leave and a reduction in the length of the work week, which hasn't dropped significantly in the last forty years.

As another strategy, the government could provide more grants and other support to artists, arts groups, nongovernment development and aid agencies, community groups and voluntary agencies. Thus someone might begin to be paid for helping to run a daycare centre, a suicide-prevention service, a senior citizens' drop-in centre or a shelter for battered women, where they had previously done this work on a voluntary basis after putting in a regular eight-hour day of, perhaps, tedious and superfluous work.

This strategy would not only meet the need for continuous income; it would also serve as a job-creation measure for the future, and perhaps a more lasting and meaningful one, through its participative design, than federal government initiatives to date. In 1982, the government had committed itself to creating 200,000 jobs; however, not even half those jobs were expected to last a year.

Education is another strategy that, by preparing people for the future, helps seed new activity within it.

I've been thinking about what to do with the rest of my life lately. Systems analyst sounds good to me. What do you think?

7
Education and Training for the Future

There is no single, fail-safe course or program of study that will equip everyone for the computerized workplaces of the future, although acquiring a general knowledge and familiarity with computer systems is a good starting point. Computer literacy is likely to become, like general literacy today, a standard prerequisite for coping in the emerging work world.

But taking one program or course in computers isn't enough. Individuals must learn to live with ongoing change. In fact, the key to success lies not in acquiring a piece of knowledge or a specific skill but in becoming flexible in the face of change that is expected to continue at least for the foreseeable future. For instance, it has been estimated that between 1979 and the end of the century, two-thirds of the content of most jobs will be replaced by different functions requiring different knowledge and skills.

Very simply, the idea of a job to last a lifetime is becoming obsolete — at least for a great many people. Hence, so is the idea of "completing" one's education. A new concept of education is needed, one emphasizing not *what* to learn, but *how* to learn. This concept describes education as an ongoing process in which individuals participate and, by doing so, learn to take charge of their own ongoing growth and development in the working world. This participative approach contrasts with the traditional view of education as a fixed prescription that one passively consumes at one sitting (albeit an extended one) usually before the age of twenty-one. Yet most people will be challenged to make this adjustment as adults, often after years of inertia within one fixed job.

Before trying to acquire and keep up with new applied skills — such as word and data processing or computerized design and computer graphics — it's useful to become computer-literate and to at least know what the core abilities are in working with computer systems. Logical problemsolving and taxonomy are two such basic abilities. Language and mathematics lie at the core of both logic and taxonomy. After all, both numbers and words are merely coded concepts; they are simply recoded into computer languages for input into computer systems where they are manipulated to solve a problem. Because of this linkage, language and mathematics are seen as vital building-block subjects for high school students preparing for a computerized work world. Physics is often stressed as well because it provides rigorous exercises in applied mathematics, although it's really necessary only for those wanting to become computer specialists.

Computer Literacy

The first element of computer literacy is learning, in basic terms, what computers do. They can store, sort, process, integrate and analyze information. But they cannot do more than they are programmed to do; they can't anticipate, except on the basis of precedent information in their memory. Similarly, they can logically deduce, but they cannot judge. Learning that computers are only as capable as they're programmed helps break down technophobia and demystify computers.

It's also important to learn the basic logic behind programming, and the limitations of what can be programmed in the first place.

For instance, the nature of programming requires the exclusion of anything that is not representable in terms of a small number of discrete choices.

Computer literacy also involves knowing something about the different types of computer communications systems (for information handling and for goods handling, for instance) and software (for calculations and for cataloguing). This prepares you for mixing and matching various system components and software in Meccano-set style to meet specific requirements.

As for the inner workings of computers, learning about assemblers, compilers, machine language and computer architecture is really only necessary for people who will become computer scientists and engineers. The majority of people won't need to know how computers work in order to use them any more than they need to know how a telephone works in order to make a call. No doubt, too, when computer communications appliances are as commonplace as the telephone, people will use them in the same blithe manner, taking for granted the immensely powerful dimension computers add to their work. This emphasis on how to use computers, rather than on how they work, is found in introductory computer courses developed at the University of Waterloo for noncomputer science students. Software programs are likened to recipes that one can pick from a cookbook-like catalogue of computer applications, ranging from the ordinary — word processing and text editing — to the complex — corporate and government information systems.

Another aspect of computer literacy involves developing a critical awareness of the new technology and its societal implications. These include the potential for disruption both in individual work lives and in entire industries, the danger of depersonalization, the loss of privacy and a decline in the quality of life, especially in a society where information can be increasingly centralized and where more and more processes are leaving the realm of human interaction to be handled, and potentially monitored, by computer systems.

This critical awareness should also include understanding the power held by those who control the computer systems. Just as a filmmaker or photographer chooses what information to leave

131

out in framing the shot, it's important to recall that excluding power is at work in the building of data banks, where what's left out can tell quite a different story than what's been included. This power is also at work in the fundamental principle — the digital, either/or principle — on which computers operate. Failing to remember this, individuals risk mistaking the computer's logic capability for human thought and reasoning. The nondigital human faculties of intuition and evaluating nuances — in other words, those aspects of human thought and judgment that cannot be quantified within the regime of computer logic — should not be underestimated. Given the tendency for people to be subtly moulded by the limitations of the technology they use, some thinkers fear that people could become more and more computer-like, increasingly comfortable thinking only in the narrow confines of either/or logic.

This is the ultimate totalitarianism: the loss of human freedom and diversity, which is to be feared and guarded against.

University and College Programs

Many aspects of computer literacy are covered in introductory computer courses provided by universities. Many offer these courses as part of their computer science curriculum and as extension courses available to part-time students at night.

Most Canadian universities have developed extension programs over the past fifteen years; however, the number of degree programs is restricted and many schools have limited offerings in working-world subjects. This leaves the majority of those who must adjust to a computer-age working environment in the midst of their working careers at a severe disadvantage, for many will lack the freedom (in terms of time and money as well as freedom from family obligations) to attend university or college full-time during the day.

At least computer courses are being increased. Fees are usually less than $100 per course, and prerequisites are often flexible, although Grade 12 or 13 remains a standard requirement for most degree courses.

In a welcome development for those who aren't able to go to the nearest campus, a number of schools (such as Mount Saint

132

Vincent University in Nova Scotia and Carleton University and Algonquin College in Ottawa) offer extension courses by television. The University of Waterloo, a trendsetter in extension education, offers courses packaged as video or audio tapes and is also experimenting with Telidon as a medium for home education. TVOntario, a provincial crown corporation devoted to instructional television, has developed a special computer literacy program, aimed at teachers and parents of school-age children.

The Centre for Continuing Education at the University of British Columbia offers a computer literacy program designed especially for women. It also features "the Knowledge Network," a province-wide telecommunications system (including satellite links) for delivering new educational material as well as for interactive, participatory education.

Distance education (or extension courses) is particularly useful for women, who make up the majority of students in this model of education delivery, largely because they're combining the schooling with child-rearing and are less free to attend campuses.

Of course, the material covered in computer extension courses varies greatly. The program at Toronto's Ryerson Polytechnical Institute includes courses leading to certificates in electronic technology, while Sudbury's Laurentian University offers a course on the impact of technology on human values and religious beliefs.

Many universities offer courses that directly fit at least some of the requirements for computer literacy — for instance, a course called "Computers in Modern Society" is available from the Open Learning Institute in Richmond, British Columbia. Alberta's Athabasca University offers a course called "Computers in Perspective."

People who are still in postsecondary education, and those who have the means to go back, have the advantage of being able to prepare for the effects of computers in their occupations rather than just reacting to them. These people also have the option to go all out for a computer profession.

While the demand for computer specialists and engineers promises to remain strong for the immediate future, the safest course may lie in a hybrid education, combining basic computer literacy with studies in health care, urban planning, accounting, library

133

science, business administration or other vocations. The majority of future jobs is likely to lie with traditional workers in the professional, paraprofessional and even support ranks, who have learned computer literacy and new applied skills, and can use them in innovative activities that will evolve from the old. While there will always be a need for computer specialists, the present high demand is likely to taper off once computer systems are installed throughout Canadian industry.

Canada's universities seem to be tailoring their programs to take account of this need for interdisciplinary education. The University of Western Ontario offers computer science programs with minors in philosophy, psychology, economics and electrical engineering. Building-block courses common to all programs there include mathematics, statistics and applied mathematics. As well, Western's School of Business Administration features mathematics and computer science as core subjects. Some typical courses include operations research, planning, information and control systems and management science. Meanwhile, at the University of New Brunswick, the manufacturing and production engineering program features courses in graphics, modelling design, systems development, computer programming and numeric control in machine tools. At various universities, students in engineering faculties are taking more courses offered by mathematics and computer science departments. However, at many schools, students will have to construct their own interdisciplinary programs.

Not all universities make their computer science curriculum into a separate department, and often degrees will be in mathematics or simply in science. Universities have usually divided computer concerns into hardware and software. The former is the province of electrical engineering and the latter, of computer science. Not surprisingly, the division has become arbitrary and loose, and often both departments offer similar instruction from different perspectives. The introductory courses offered will cover many aspects of computer literacy. In other disciplines relevant courses can be found — for instance, a course in business information systems from a business administration program. It's worth shopping around to see what various schools have to offer.

Computer science studies typically include a handful of core

134

subjects: mathematics; problemsolving by computer (the problems may be business-related, mathematical or scientific); computer systems and machine structure, which can involve detailed study of microcomputers; data communications and networks, for computer communications applications; and computer languages. Other subjects that might be included would range from communications and networks to systems analysis in organization and management.

Just what courses people in noncomputer fields would pick out of a curriculum depends a lot on how computers are being used in their fields. Someone pursuing a career in teaching might select courses on the role of computer communications technology in education, or on the rudiments of software and programming languages, or on Telidon graphics. Students with a bent for organization and an interest in management and administration might orient themselves toward managing computer information systems and systems requirements in the office and factory of the future by taking courses in management and business administration as well as in computer systems design and implementation.

At the community college level, many of the same core subjects are offered as at universities, but with the emphasis on practical application or computer principles rather than the theory informing them. Of course, the explicit objective of community college programs is to place people in jobs — in this case, the technical and professional jobs described in Chapter 6.

Typical of college offerings is Algonquin College in Ottawa, which has a three-year program leading to a diploma in computer or electronics engineering technology, a two-year diploma program in electronic engineering drafting, a two-year program in data processing in general business and one-year certificate programs in information processing, electronics and digital equipment (to train technicians) and accelerated electronics.

Degree programs for technologists at polytechnical institutes (like Ryerson in Toronto and the Northern and Southern Alberta Institutes of Technology) and diploma programs at community colleges provide a solid grounding not only in electronics but also in building-block subjects such as physics and mathematics. They

135

also include instruction in building electronic circuits, using data processing and using computers in design and drafting work.

At NAIT, in Alberta — which also offers apprenticeship programs, including one for electronics technicians, requiring only a Grade 10 education — there are three programs centred on computer communications technology, each requiring two years of study. One is in computer systems technology, a second is in electrical engineering technology, and another is in telecommunications engineering technology. Interestingly, computer concepts and skills are also incorporated in a number of other programs, including accounting, administrative management and marketing management and health-record technology.

At community colleges, technician-level single-year courses in electronics focus on operating techniques and specific equipment, rather than operating principles. Typical subjects might include soldering, basic electronics and VDT service.

An advantage of the polytechnical programs is that in combining the theoretical aspects of a university education with vocational training, they produce graduates who are able to implement computer systems as well as run and maintain them. This creates an alternative to the traditional hierarchy of personnel in industry, where the theoretical people are at the top and the applied-science people are below with relatively little prospect of occupational mobility.

Besides public postsecondary institutions, it is worthwhile investigating semiprivate educational programs run by professional associations such as the Canadian Bankers' Association. With the momentum of their own self-interest augmented by their own funding, they can sometimes respond to new educational demands faster than the larger and more bureaucratic public institutions. Not all of these institutions have unquestioned and wide credibility, however. As well, some that are run by firms selling the computer equipment itself can handicap graduates by restricting them to only one line of equipment.

Keeping abreast of a subject area requires new strategies in self-education. One strategy would be joining professional associations; another encompasses an expanded role for unions in education

136

and training; subscribing to journals, attending conferences and taking extension courses are other useful strategies.

Self-help groups such as the women's networks springing up in cities across Canada (including a national one to share information on computer-related issues) and women's resource centres, in Montreal, Hamilton, Vancouver and other cities, offer other means for women to confront the socialization that leads them to see support work as conducive to the wife-mother role, as their primary role in life. Through drop-in chats and weekend workshops, women can help each other identify and overcome their self-image handicap. As well, an experimental program at Ryerson in Toronto is combining this self-help concept with instruction in computer literacy within a package designed for women returning to the work force after raising families. The program integrates community discussion groups with classroom instruction in computers, change management, research skills and problemsolving.

Education for Canadians

Thus far we've looked at what individuals can do to prepare themselves for the changing employment market and, by knowing how to work with computer technology and put it to new uses, help to trigger or hasten the innovation phase of computerization. But individual action won't take care of the larger problem: the disarray of government and industry in making these preparations on a national scale. Essentially, industry's training extends only to new applied skills, not to teaching the operating principles and procedures of whole new systems — the kind of thing community and technical colleges do — or the underlying theory, which one learns at university.

As the country's chronic short-handedness in some skilled trades has shown, Canadian educational policy has to become more flexible and more responsive to the changing needs of industry. This calls for greater federal–provincial cooperation both in monitoring industry needs and in designing intelligent training and educational strategies to meet those needs. Certainly industry itself doesn't seem capable of keeping up with its need for trained personnel. A 1981 parliamentary study on Canada's skill needs for the 1980s found that only 20 percent of industry was providing training. As well, a 1976 federal government study that surveyed industry's views on skill needs arising from anticipated technological changes found that the majority of industries *at that time* considered that their existing training programs wouldn't be adequate to meet the retraining needs they anticipated.

Unfortunately, both levels of government fail as they compete with each other, both in interpreting industry's demands and in defining goals for postsecondary education and training. The provinces regard education as their exclusive jurisdiction, but the federal government considers postsecondary education and training as its preserve. To this confusion can be added the federal government's determination to continue cutbacks in social program transfer payments to the provinces, which is all too certain to result in a decline in the quality of education and the shelving of new initiatives such as computer literacy programs. Furthermore, it shouldn't concentrate its assistance on applied-skills training, but should support a much broader education; for learning how to work in a computerized information or manufacturing system provides a solid base on which one can quickly learn new application skills as the continuing advance of technology creates new skill needs and consigns old skills to the dustbin.

In the area of immediate professional skill needs, a shortfall of engineers and applied scientists, mentioned in Chapter 6, is projected. There is also a pressing need to expand programs for technologists and technicians such as data processors, computer technicians, word processors and information systems technologists. And we need more public education, too; while other countries have poured millions of dollars a year into computer literacy and public awareness programs about computer communications since the 1970s, the Canadian government has limited its role to boosting the manufacture of the technology itself.

Against this background it's hard to be optimistic about the nature of government response to the challenges that lie ahead. For individuals to respond with any effectiveness, particularly in the midst of their working lives, educational-leave opportunities must be greatly expanded. This was a key recommendation in a major government study called *Education and Working Canadians*, published by Labour Canada in 1979. The study also recommended that the cost of re-education and retraining be distributed more equitably both among industries and between industry and government — in other words, that industry should pay more. This could be achieved through cooperative work-study programs, or job-sharing programs modified to include the principle of educational leave and apprenticeship, which itself could be expanded to take in new white-collar technical and paraprofessional job areas such as programming, information brokerage, packaging and management.

Another problem to be reckoned with is the high proportion of the adult Canadian population that is functionally illiterate: about one in four adults, according to the 1981 parliamentary task force. Another 1981 report noted that as of 1976, 25 percent of adult Ontarians had less than a Grade 9 education, and a quarter of a million people had less than Grade 5. This suggests that many of the people needing to be retrained as automation takes over their jobs in mines, processing plants, factories and offices might have difficulty comprehending written instructional material.

Women are handicapped with an additional form of illiteracy: a lack of science background from school days when they felt more comfortable taking "domestic" courses, such as home economics. Not having taken the tough career preparation courses, such as enriched mathematics and physics, women are unprepared for the new, more technical and math-related requirements of computer-age jobs. This under-representation in school science classes and later in college and university, and on faculties and in science professions, is identified as a major contemporary problem in a 1982 Science Council of Canada report, *Who Turns the Wheel*. It recommends special measures to encourage high school girls to take the math and science subjects. But working women need special help as well. One solution might be to have universities and colleges offer extension coures in remedial science and mathematics not only restricted to female students but designed for them as well. For instance, research has found that while males learn abstract mathematical concepts well, females grasp the material best when it is presented within a framework of the larger social context.

Education is only one aspect of survival in the computer age. Protecting your job and your rights in the workplace are perhaps the most critical aspects.

I'm afraid Mr. Harris is no longer with us. He was phased out by a chip no bigger than the head of a pin.

8

In the Workplace

T here is only so much that in-
dividuals can do on their own in confronting the challenges and
hazards of the computer revolution. Collective measures, taken
by a group as a union, or on behalf of a group by legislation and
other government measures, might be needed as well. For instance, a company might be reluctant to take on the additional
cost of providing retraining for redundant clerical staff unless its
competitors are forced to carry similar overhead costs themselves.

Unions and Legislative Protection

Unions, of course, cannot do anything directly for those Canadians
who aren't organized, and the majority are not. Nationally, 43
percent of working men and 27 percent of women are unionized.
This gap between the sexes has been narrowing: the number of
unionized women doubled between 1966 and 1976. But attempts
to close it have run into formidable hurdles in some of the tra-

ditional female job ghettos. Only 16 percent of office workers outside public administration are union members. As well, Canada's giant banks, with fewer than a hundred branches organized in 1981, are among the strongest resisters of unionization. One has generated so many complaints to labour relations boards of unfair labour practices that a separate category of complaints has been set up exclusively for the banks.

Even for those who are in unions, membership does not provide ironclad protection against technological change. A hundred telephone operators in Quebec seemed well protected when Bell Canada decided to shut down their jobs by closing four regional offices in the spring of 1981. Their contract provided for possible redundancy due to technological change, and since the closings were a centralization move made possible by the automation of long-distance phoning, they qualified for retraining and transfers to other jobs. However, few women received meaningful training, and the guarantee of job transfers applied only for transfers to other operator positions, which, in a line of work hit hard by automation, were understandably hard to find. Of forty-one redundant operators at one regional centre, only sixteen received transfers.

Part of the problem was attitude. The company appeared to regard operators not as valuable members of an organization, but simply as production costs and even impediments to increased productivity. Observance of its contract obligations to them, therefore, was grudging and token. When the union, the Canadian Federation of Communications Workers, subsequently entered new contract talks, it was determined to increase members' protection against that attitude with more provisions for technological change, and it won the right to consultation on technological change through special labour–management committees.

Yet the existing protection in the contract would compare favourably with most other labour agreements. In a 1978 study of more than a thousand collective agreements covering workers under federal and provincial jurisdictions — done by the Carrothers Commission of Inquiries into Redundancies and Layoffs for Labour Canada — most agreements were found to have no provisions for technological change. Fewer than 20 percent provided any wage

144

or employment guarantee or called for a labour–management committee to deal with technological change. Fewer than 3 percent provided for a relocation allowance. Fewer than 30 percent called for training or retraining. And only 44 percent of the contracts provided for severance pay and supplementary unemployment insurance.

These provisions have been won in a climate of government indifference, at best, to employees' rights in regard to technological change. For unionized workers, certain rights are spelled out in the Canada Labour Code, which applies to employees in the federal government and its Crown corporations, and in the labour acts of Manitoba, Saskatchewan and British Columbia, where the labour-sympathetic New Democratic Party has held office. These rights are minimum advance notice (generally ninety days) and renegotiation of contract relationships such as seniority that will be affected by the technological change. In Saskatchewan and British Columbia, however, if these renegotiations are fruitless, the legislation provides for the right to strike as a contingency.

For nonunionized workers, there is no legislative protection anywhere. The legislation for union workers doesn't spell out what constitutes technological change — for instance, whether it begins with changing the organization of work in the standardization phase, which has been identified as a necessary precondition of automation. Nor does it say what aspects of technological change are negotiable — for instance, can the means of implementing the technology and the choice of equipment be discussed, in addition to retraining and relocation for displaced workers? Nor does the legislation establish a standard for responsibility regarding technological change — specifying, for instance, that someone who has invested a number of years and skill and energy in a certain workplace has accumulated certain rights, such as the right to continuous employment, a chance for retraining or at least fair severance pay and pension protection.

Some of these questions have been addressed in the two major government inquiries that have been conducted on technological change. The report by Justice Samuel Freedman in 1964 recommended that any significant technological change be the subject of collective bargaining, with unions allowed access to strike action

145

to protect their interests. More recently, the Carrothers commission recommended in its 1979 report that employers be obliged to consult with unions regarding the implementation of technological change and that they also be held responsible for retraining and re-employment. But the federal government has made no move to adopt any of these measures; if anything, it has weakened workers' protection against the negative consequences of automation in recent years, through a series of restrictions on unemployment insurance.

Despite government inaction on technological change and the at best mixed success in contract negotiations to date, unions have certainly not given up on this issue. The Canadian arm of the United Steelworkers of America, one of the country's largest unions, adopted a technological "bill of rights" at its 1981 policy conference. It challenges the traditional management prerogative to control technological change exclusively. It also asserts that workers are subjects, not objects, in a work process and have a right to be involved in implementing new technology.

The Steelworkers' bill of rights calls for at least two years' advance notice of impending change, complete disclosure on the changes contemplated, worker participation and, most important, *approval* of the planning and implementation of the change. The Canadian Labour Congress adopted a similar bill of rights regarding technological change at its national policy conference early in 1982.

These policies fundamentally challenge the tradition of management having exclusive control over the design of jobs and the organization of work, including the implementation of technological change. If they succeed in replacing that exclusive prerogative with joint labour–management control over computerization, with workers participating in job redesign and training decisions, among other implementation measures, they could become an enabling factor for continuing employment into the innovation phase of applying the technology.

The idea of workers having rights in the organization of work and in changes affecting their employment is an accepted feature of industrial relations in West Germany and some Scandinavian countries. Called industrial democracy, these rights include con-

146

tinuity of employment, with training and occupational bridging used as strategies to carry out that right, as well as the right to work in an environment free from health and safety hazards.

Health and Safety

Unions have also spoken out on the health issues that arise from work at VDTs, issues that, while quite different in nature from technological redundancy, nevertheless relate to the basic question of how the technology is applied. For the problems that have been identified relate as much to the organization of VDT jobs as to the machines themselves.

Various studies have found that health problems can result from work in word processing pools where only one task is performed, relentlessly. A Swedish study of operators of computer terminals, word processors and related equipment found that 75 percent of the workers had developed eye trouble, 55 percent had back problems and 35 percent had headaches.

While such problems have been around as long as there has been sedentary work, psychological stress among word processor operators is more clearly a product of the computer age. An informal study of word processor operators working in a large centralized word processing centre in the federal government found high rates of absenteeism and of sedative use. Some women regularly burst into tears; others chattered to their machines. A 1980 report by the International Labour Organization describes these symptoms as a distinctive psychopathology associated with the rationalization, centralization and deskilling found in many large word processing centres. The victims are suffering from monotony, isolation and productivity pressure, as well as lack of autonomy, variety and growth opportunities in their work.

It seems that the white-collar world can no longer be assumed to be a congenial, let alone a safe, place to work.

Perhaps the biggest question about VDT safety hinges on the effects of the various types of radiation given off by the cathode-ray tubes in VDTs, namely x-rays, ultraviolet and infrared light and microwave radiation. This last form of radiation has been shown to induce cataracts, sterility, nausea, changes in heart patterns and blood changes that produce leukemia, a Toronto conference on this issue was told.

In Canada, the greatest concern has been that radiation may be responsible for birth defects in children whose mothers operated VDTs while pregnant. A number of unions formed a VDT ad hoc committee in 1980, after four women who worked with VDTs in the *Toronto Star*'s classified advertising department had babies with birth defects, and it has been successful in bringing public attention to this issue. In 1981, the Communications Workers of Canada won a landmark agreement endorsing the right of pregnant equipment operators to refuse to work on VDTs. The concession resulted from Labour Canada's investigation of the VDTs used by Bell Canada for possible radiation. It was launched after four pregnant operators refused to work on the equipment on the grounds that doing so constituted an imminent danger to their health — grounds sanctioned under the Canada Labour Code.

Elsewhere, the problems of physical stress and psychological distress have been addressed as well. In Sweden, union contracts for word processing and data processing operators now require ten- or fifteen-minute rest periods every hour and regular employer-paid eye examinations. The government has laid down guidelines for terminal equipment, workstation configuration and background lighting. In Norway, where contract protections similar to Sweden's prevail, a regulation has been proposed that would prohibit anyone from being required to work more than half of the day in front of a VDT.

The Electronic Cottage

Concerns about the physical and psychological effects of heavy VDT use are also raised in conjunction with working at home, which is making a comeback now that the home can be turned into an "electronic cottage" by the installation of a computer terminal.

Control Data, a large, innovative computer systems firm with headquarters in the United States and offices in Canada, has 100 participants in an electronic cottage project, called the Alternate Worksite Program. The workers range from professionals to support staff. In a paper prepared for a conference on electronic information systems, the project was described as an opportunity to tap into the homebound labour force. Besides handicapped individuals, the paper noted, "one large untapped labour market is composed of mothers . . . ." It goes on to list among other benefits the opportunity to conserve energy — a factor that can be expected to encourage further the work-at-home idea — as well as the opportunity to "reduce the operating and overhead costs of an organization" (by letting the home worker assume them, presumably).

Those with strong bargaining power — home-based professional consultants, for instance — would probably be more successful than the less skilled and thus more replaceable word and data processors at building overhead costs into their fees or wages. As well, someone whose relative poverty is already reflected in cramped living quarters would be less able to take on this work than someone who can simply install the equipment in a spare bedroom.

Home work could very easily become a new confining characteristic of "women's work," a new female job ghetto, and it could happen very quickly. Home work lends itself readily to the clerical and service work that women have traditionally done. Computer monitoring cuts out the need for personal supervision. And special working or operating instructions can be relayed as computer-aided instruction.

As automated teller machines proliferate, one can imagine the banks exploring the home-based work option, or a similar option of satellite service centres, for providing telephone back-up service to those banking facilities. There is also a wide potential for home-based telephone-terminal back-up to videotex services such as tele-shopping. As was seen in Chapter 3, the Continental Bank in the United States has already installed terminals in clerical workers' homes and channels dictation work to them there, although the women, interviewed for *Business Week* magazine, complained about feeling isolated and lonely stuck behind their home terminals. The article didn't specify whether returning to their office and joining the larger picture was an option available to these workers. Nor did it say on what basis the women were being paid. In at least one work-at-home project, in West Germany, the participants are paid on a piecework basis.

This method of payment underscores and reinforces the isolation associated with single-function jobs such as word processing and, in general, the formation of job ghettos. The worker is effectively devalued to the basis of the quantity of words or whatever that he or she can produce. There is no provision for quality, no acknowledgment of a whole person who might want to learn new things and take on fresh challenges. Cut off from social contact, distanced from the opportunity to demonstrate potential and to find out about new-job potential in the larger office, isolated within the four walls of home and condemned to a one-dimensional identity (line-count per day or hour), women could find themselves losing much of the ground they've gained over the past fifty years.

Government guidelines to protect home-based workers are urgently needed, especially since the work situation by definition thwarts the possibility of collective action. These workers, especially those in the support category, may not even know who their fellows are, let alone come in contact with them to compare notes on work situations.

Quality of Working Life

There is yet another means of addressing the employment concerns raised by technological change. Here, workers and management participate jointly in designing jobs and overall systems within which jobs are performed. Called Quality of Working Life (QWL) and sometimes participative management, this relatively new concept greatly enhances the scope of industrial relations, which has traditionally been constrained, at least in North America, by confrontational labour–management postures and a focus narrowly confined to existing jobs and working conditions.

QWL is founded on the belief that organizations work more effectively when the people working in them have some say in how they are designed and operated. Its purpose, therefore, is to redefine jobs and the overall organization of work in a way that enhances worker participation in the operating system. In specific terms, this involves allowing workers more autonomy and decisionmaking responsibility than has been associated with the traditional view of workers as merely units of labour, and antagonistic units at that.

Rather than concentrating on units of labour, QWL stresses people's social needs in the work environment. For instance, studies in the QWL field maintain that people's willingness to accept responsibility is determined to a large extent by the amount of control allocated to them. Related needs include a sense of belonging, a sense of relevance — meaning that one's work is contributing something to the larger social welfare — as well as the need for variety, challenge and a desirable future to inspire commitment and effort — in short, the opposite of a dead-end job.

Not surprisingly, QWL is more accepted in Europe, which has an established tradition of industrial democracy, than in North America, which doesn't. Still, there are examples where it has been accepted and borne fruit, and Canadian government bodies such as the Ontario Quality of Working Life Centre are promoting QWL in industry.

Irving Bluestone was one of the early pioneers of QWL when, as director of the United Auto Workers General Motors Department, he signed the first national QWL agreement in the United States in 1973. Based on collaboration and cooperation rather than confrontation, QWL changes attitudes through the dialogue that goes on in it. A sharply lowered number of local disputes and grievances has been credited to the QWL process at GM over the years. As well, in 1979, half a dozen locals settled their problems even before the national contract was concluded, another breakthrough that has been credited to QWL.

A review of QWL programs within the Canadian federal government noted that while the innovative approach might involve a temporary increase in costs, it should reduce costs in the long run through reductions in absenteeism, turnover and wastage. For instance, a QWL project among data-entry clerks in Statistics Canada led to a decrease in unscheduled leave and turnover.

One private industry success story is a QWL project at Shell Canada's head office word processing centre. Staff participated in a major redrafting of work procedures and a physical reorganization of the centre. The substitution of self-regulating work groups

151

for highly structured central control resulted in increased job satisfaction and higher productivity.

Ultimately, for QWL to be meaningful, it must reverse the central principle on which jobs have been defined since the industrial revolution: the reductionist principle. Work is divided into two phases: first, initiative and innovative work and second, the production, application and fulfillment of the initiative phase. Once this initial distinction has been made, there is a successive division of the production phase into component jobs and tasks, which are progressively segmented, fragmented, simplified, standardized and finally routinized and trivialized to the point that they're either automated or, perhaps, assigned to a social scientist for superficial recombination in job redesign projects dressed up as QWL, instead of reintegrating the process function with the initiative or control function for true participatory management.

In a paper published in *Control Systems* magazine, a British engineer, Howard Rosenbrock, speculated on the origin of this relentless divide-and-conquer process and wondered how engineers could escape from the world-view that condemned them to serve it continuously. He felt that the world-view itself prevents engineers from seeing technology as a means of enhancing rather than replacing people and from conceiving ways of applying technology in an enhancing way. He ended by suggesting that if there isn't a new approach, there is at least a growing disillusionment with the values that lead to segmentation, fragmentation, deskilling and mass unemployment due to automation, and that this is at least a beginning.

Afterword

Not long after finishing the manuscript for this book, I gave a speech not only about automation but also about the training, education and other adjustments required for Canadians to find new work in new applications of computer technology. During the question period, someone asked me why I wasn't challenging the role of computer technology itself. I agreed with the need to address the "why" of computers in our society; however, I said, it seemed to be my duty as a speaker to discuss what people can do about the technology now, as it is currently affecting their lives. Hence, I felt it was my responsibility to discuss practical responses to the technology — such as training, adult education and technological change clauses in collective agreements, as well as specific legislation to prevent exploitation, discrimination and physical and mental suffering through computer use, to protect personal privacy, to ensure a diversity of information sources and to counter corporate concentration.

These are the tools at our disposal, and we must make use of them, I said. In doing so, not only do we take charge of the technology, but we can then direct it toward shared human goals — such as enhancing what people do and enriching their lives and freedom rather than replacing, deskilling or otherwise diminishing them. By understanding computers, by knowing how to work with them, and by participating in their implementation, I believe we can enlarge our power in relation to this technology.

Someone then commented that I seemed to be very optimistic. I am *determined* to be optimistic, I said.

If we don't master this technology as a tool, we will be mastered by its ends and subjugated to its technique.

Sources and
Suggested Readings

Preface

An interesting historical analysis of the industrial revolution is provided in Karl Polanyi's *The Great Transformation: The Political and Economic Origins of Our Time* (Boston: Beacon Press, 1965). Joseph Weizenbaum, a computer scientist with MIT, provides a thoughtful discussion on the philosophical and political implications of computer technology in *Computer Power and Human Reason: From Judgement to Calculation* (San Francisco: MIT Press/W.H. Freeman & Co., 1976). Daniel Bell's *The Coming of the Post-Industrial Society: A Venture in Social Forecasting* (New York: Basic Books, 1973) is a valuable contribution. Also of interest is "Engineers and the Work that People Do," by H.H. Rosenbrock, in the electrical engineering journal *Technology and Society* (Vol. 9, No. 3). Among Canadian contributions, I recommend George Thompson's essay *Memo from Mercury: Information Technology Is Different* (Halifax: The Institute for Research on Public Policy, 1979) and *The Infor-*

mation Revolution and Its Implications for Canada, by S. Serafini and M. Andrieu (Hull: Supply and Services Canada, 1980).

Chapter 1

On the history of computers, some sources of particular note are Christopher Evans's book, *The Micro Millennium* (New York: Washington Square Press, 1979); and, among Canadian sources, "The Effects of Microelectronics on Employment and Income," a 1980 discussion paper by Katherine McGuire for the Canadian Labour Congress; and *The Microelectronic Revolution*, by Lydia Dotto (Toronto: Housser & Co. Ltd., 1981). Finally, *Computer Consciousness: Surviving the Automated 80s*, by H. Dominic Covvey and Neil Harding McAlister (Don Mills: Addison-Wesley, 1980), is an excellent introduction to computer technology.

Chapter 2

Some useful material on the hardware of the automated office includes "Automating Offices from Top to Bottom: A Special Report," in *Electronics* (March 10, 1981); and "Office Information Systems," a special issue of the IEEE Computer Society journal *Computer* (May 1981). Canadian sources include Sharon Coates's *The Office of the Future* (Ottawa: Department of Communications, 1980); *The Electronic Office in Canada* (Ottawa: Department of Communications, 1982); Chapter 2 of *Women and the Chip: Case Studies of Informatics on Employment in Canada*, by Heather Menzies (Montreal: Institute for Research on Public Policy, 1981); Robert Arnold Russell's *The Electronic Briefcase: The Office of the Future* (Montreal: IRPP, 1978); and Don Tapscott's "Investigating the Office of the Future," in *Telesis*, the house organ of Bell Northern Research (Vol. 8, No. 1).

Some of the best and most current research on the employment effects of office automation has been done in Canada. Of particular note are three studies published by the Institute for Research on Public Policy (IRPP). In historical order, they are: *The Impacts of Computer/Communications on Employment in Canada: An Overview of OECD Debates*, prepared by Zavis Zeman (Montreal: IRPP, 1979); *Women and the Chip: Case Studies of Informatics on Employment in Canada*, by Heather Menzies (Montreal: IRPP, 1981); and *Microelectronics and Employment in Public Administration: Three Ontario Municipalities, 1970-1980*, by Russell Wilkins (Montreal: IRPP, 1981). Also of interest are two publications from the Science Council of Canada: *The Impact of the Microelectronics Revolution on Work and Working* (Ottawa: Science Council of Canada, 1980) and *Planning for an Information Society: Tomorrow is Too Late* (Ottawa: Science Council of Canada, 1982). Good sources outside Canada include "Race Against Time: Automation of the Office," a report that explores trends in office automation and the impact on the office workforce, prepared by Working Women, National Association of Office Workers (Cleveland, Ohio; 1980); *The Impact of Chip Technology on Employment and the Labour Market*, by the Metra Consulting Group (London, 1980); *The Future with Microelectronics*, by Iann Barron and Ray Curnow (London: Frances Printer Ltd., 1979); and "The Effect of Technological and Structural Changes on the Employment and Working Conditions of Non-Manual Workers," by the Advisory Committee on Salaried Employees and Professional Workers of the International Labour Organization (Geneva, 1981).

Chapter 3

Chapters 4 through 6 of Menzies, *Women and the Chip*, provide new research and summarize existing information on automation in banks, insurance and supermarkets. Additional insights on employment shifts in the insurance industry are provided in Stephen Peitchinis's report, *The Employment Implications of Computers and Telecommunications Technology* (Ottawa: Supply and Services Canada, 1981). On library automation, see Steven Globerman's *The Adoption of Computer Technology in Selected Canadian Service Industries* (Ottawa: Economic Council of Canada, 1981), which also examines automation trends in Canadian hospitals and retail trade. On automation in the telephone industry, see Joan Newman Kuyek's *The Phone Book: Working at the Bell* (Kitchener: Between the Lines, 1979); "Memorandum of Evidence to the Canadian Industrial Communications Assembly Regarding Technological Change and Productivity and a Rate Increase Application by Bell Canada," presented to the Canadian Radio-television and Telecommunications Commission (Ottawa, 1981) by Harry Strahl; and "The Potential for Telecommunicating," in *Business Week* (January 26, 1981). Other *Business Week* articles used as sources include "Supermarket Scanners Get Smarter" (August 17, 1981) and "Putting the Library on a Computer" (March 30, 1981). On supermarket automation, see also Bill Reno's article "Supermarket Technology," in *The Canadian Forum* (March 1982), and "Disappearing Jobs: The Impact of Computers on Employment," by Bruce Gilchrist and Arlaana Shenkin in *The Futurist* (February 1981).

Chapter 4

Good sources on the technology of factory automation include two articles from the IEEE magazine *Spectrum*: "Busy Robots Spur Productivity" (September 1979) and "The Blue Collar Robot" (September 1980). Other sources include "Japanese Rush to Robot Production," in *Electronics* (October 6, 1981) and a special report on computers in the March 8, 1980, issue of *The Financial Post*. See also "Computer-Aided Design," in the IEEE Computer Society's *Computer Graphics and Applications* (April 1981). For an overview of Canada's situation in factory automation, see *Strategy for Survival: Issues and Recommendations Concerning the Implementation and Impact of CAD/CAM Technology in Canadian Industry* (Ottawa: Department of Industry, Trade and Commerce, 1980) and *The Weakest Link: A Technological Perspective on Canadian Industrial Underdevelopment*, by John Britton and James Gilmour (Ottawa: Science Council of Canada, 1978). For information on the employment implications, see the following: *Metalworkers and New Technology: Results of IMF Questionnaire on Industrial Robots*, published by the International Metalworkers' Federation (Document 81-13, Geneva); and three articles in the December 1981 issue of *Canadian Dimension*: "Numerical Control," by Harley Shaiken; "Who Pays?" by Frank Emspack; and "The Spectre of the Silicon Chip," by Barry Diacon. Two Canadian sources are C.A. Jecchinis's *The Impact of Microelectronic Technology on Employment: A Survey of Current Research Studies in Selected West European Countries*, published in 1980 by the Labour Market Research Unit of the Ontario

Manpower Commission in Toronto; and Colin Moorhouse's "Technological and Systems Change," a 1980 study paper sponsored by the British Columbia Regional Education Department of the Canadian Labour Congress. Two more studies on employment effects are *The Manpower Implications of Microelectronic Technology*, by Jonathan Sleigh and Brian Boatwright (London: Government of Great Britain, 1979); and the European Trade Union Institute's *The Impact of Microelectronics on Employment in Western Europe in the 1980s* (Brussels: Gunter Kopke, 1980).

Chapter 5

There are a number of good Canadian sources on videotex, particularly on the Canadian technology, Telidon. These include a 1979 study by H.G. Bown, C.D. O'Brien, W. Sawchuk and J.R. Storey for the Communications Research Centre of the federal government's Department of Communications, *Picture Description Instructions (PDI) for the Telidon Videotex System*; Fernande Faulkner and Michael Gurstein, *Telidon and Its Applications* (proceedings of a seminar, September 1980), a 1981 report by Socioscope Inc. of Ottawa; *Gutenberg Two: The New Electronics and Social Change*, edited by Dave Godfrey and Douglas Parkhill (Toronto: Press Porcépic, 1979); and a 1980 Infomart report, edited by Richard Larratt, *Inside Videotex: The Future . . . Now* (proceedings of a seminar, March 1980). See also "Planning the Videotex Network," by J.M. Costa and A.M. Chitnis, in *Canadian Electronics Engineering* (April 1980); and "Where is Videotex Going?" by Darby Miller in *Data Communications* (September 1981). On the corporate developments, see "The Race to Plug In," in *Business Week* (December 8, 1980); "The Economics of Canadian Broadcasting," by S. McFadyen, C. Hoskins and D. Gillen in *Canadian Broadcasting: Market Structure and Economic Performance* (Halifax: Institute for Research on Public Policy, 1980); and the report *Royal Commission on Newspapers* (Ottawa: Supply and Services Canada, 1981). On computer-aided instruction, see "The Big RED/GREEN/BLUE Schoolhouse: Videotex and Learning in the '80s," a paper given by C.W. Brahan and W.D. Godfrey at the Viewdata-81 Conference at London in October 1981, and "Learning and Technology:

159

Dangers and Opportunities," a paper given by Peter S. Sindell at the IMPACT Learning and Technology conference, jointly sponsored by the Canadian Association for Adult Education and the Ontario Association for Continuing Education, held in Toronto in 1981. Also of note are two articles in the July 27, 1981, issue of *Business Week*: "On-the-Job Training by Computer" and "School Computers Score at Last."

Chapter 6

Some sources used in this chapter that provide useful further reading are *Skills and Shortages: A Summary Guide to the Findings of the Human Resources Survey*, by Gordon Betcherman (Ottawa: Economic Council of Canada, 1980); *Informatics: Occupational Analysis Series*, a report by Occupational and Career Analysis Development at Employment and Immigration Canada (Ottawa: Supply and Services Canada, 1980); *The Impact of the Microelectronics Industry on the Structure of the Canadian Economy*, by Michael J. McLean (Montreal: IRPP, 1979); and "Office Information Systems," in *Computer* (May 1981).

Chapter 7

In addition to the calendars of universities and colleges across Canada, see *Computer-Aided Design and Manufacturing in Canada*, a 1977 report published by the federal Department of Industry, Trade and Commerce that includes a listing of educational institutions and research organizations in this area. On policy issues, see three government reports: *Work for Tomorrow: Employment Opportunities for the '80s*, the report of a parliamentary task force (Ottawa: House of Commons, 1981); *Labour Market Development in the 1980s*, the report of a task force at Employment and Immigration Canada (Ottawa, 1981); and the report of the Commission of Inquiry on Educational Leave and Productivity, *Education and Working Canadians*, by R. J. Adams (Ottawa: Supply and Services Canada, 1979). In addition, regarding women and technology training, see Menzies's *Computer Technology and the Education of Female Students* (Ottawa: The Canadian Teachers' Federation, 1982); and *Who Turns the Wheel*, an excellent report on the under-representation of women in technology-related careers and the prerequisite education (Ottawa: Science Council of Canada, 1982).

Chapter 8

For an overview of technological change protection in Canadian union contracts and under Canadian labour legislation, see two papers: "The Effects of Microelectronics on Employment and Income," by Katherine McGuire, prepared for the Canadian Labour Congress (Ottawa, 1980); and "Legislative Analysis on Provisions Relating to Technological Change and Group Termination," prepared for the Race Against Time conference of the National Union of Provincial Government Employees (Ottawa, March 1982). Two good discussions of possible strategies in response to technological change are *The Implications of Microelectronics for Canadian Workers* by Boris Mather, Jane Stinson and George Warskett (Ottawa: The Canadian Centre for Policy Alternatives, 1981) and *Technological Change and Work* (Ottawa: The Canadian Labour Congress, 1982). On women's employment concerns, see Julie White's *Women and Unions* (Ottawa: Advisory Council on the Status of Women, 1980). On health hazard questions, see Bob de Matteo's *The Hazards of VDTs* (Toronto: Ontario Public Service Employees Union, 1981); Linda Rosenbaum's "Health Effects of Video Display Terminals: The Non-Radiation Problems," a 1981 report from the Health Advocacy Unit at the City of Toronto's Department of Public Health; and *Potential Health Effects of VDTs and Radio Frequency Heaters and Sealers*, which are the proceedings from hearings before the Subcommittee on Investigations and Oversight, Committee of Science and Technology, U.S. House of Representatives (Washington, 1981).

On QWL concerns, see Calvin Pava's *Microprocessor Technology and the Quality of Working Life: Prospects for Organizational Choice Amid Technological Revolution*, a 1981 report to the Ontario Ministry of Labour's Quality of Working Life Centre; David Jenkins's *QWL — Current Trends and Directions* (Toronto: Ontario Quality of Working Life Centre, 1981); and "QWL in the Federal Public Service," transcript of a presentation by Dr. Eric Trist and Dr. William A. Westley to the Senior Steering Committee on QWL in the Federal Public Service (Ottawa, 1981).